lonely planet

Diving & Snorkeling

Baja California

Walt Peterson

LONELY PLANET PUBLICATIONS
Melbourne • Oakland • London • Paris

Diving & Snorkeling Baja California
- A Lonely Planet Pisces Book

1st Edition
February, 1999

Published by
Lonely Planet Publications
192 Burwood Road, Hawthorn, Victoria 3122, Australia

Other offices
150 Linden Street, Oakland, California 94607, USA
10A Spring Place, London NW5 3BH, UK
1 rue du Dahomey, 75011 Paris, France

Photographs by photographers as indicated

Front cover photograph
Whale shark and diver, by Tammy Peluso

Back cover photographs
by Kenneth Howard, Tammy Peluso, Walt Stearns

ISBN 0 86442 572 4

text and maps © Lonely Planet 1999
photographs © photographers as indicated 1999
John Elliott Thayer illustration courtesy of the Peabody Essex
Museum, Salem, Mass. Photo by Mark Sexton

Printed by H&Y Printing Ltd., Hong Kong

Although the author
and publisher have tried
to make the information
as accurate as possible,
they accept no respon-
sibility for any loss,
injury or inconvenience
sustained by any person
using this book.

Contents

Author

Walt Peterson

Walt has engineering degrees from the U.S. Coast Guard Academy and Rensselaer Polytechnic Institute, and a master's in systems management from the University of Southern California. He was a career Coast Guard officer, serving on an icebreaker, an ocean station vessel and in civil engineering and management positions. He retired in 1978. He made his first dive in 1949 and has explored many of the world's great dive sites, including the Great Barrier Reef, Sipadan, Walindi, Sulawesi, Komodo and the Red Sea, but Baja and the Sea of Cortez have brought him back over 50 times. This is his fourth book.

From the Author

I would like to thank my wife Judy, who spent hundreds of hours helping to develop the cartography and reading the manuscript; my brother Reeve Peterson and my son Michael, both of whom served as drivers, divers, boat crew, explorers, cooks and dishwashers during many diving trips to Baja; to Georgia and Suzy Peterson, my sister-in-law and niece, respectively, who cheerfully accommodated many overnight house guests en route to and returning from Baja; and to Mimy Eng, who participated in several information-gathering trips.

Thanks are also due to Alex Kerstitch and Daniel Gotshall, marine biologists and authors, who reviewed the sections on marine life; to editors Roslyn Bullas and Debra Miller at Lonely Planet, both of whom kept everything heading in the right direction; and to Alex Guilbert and Bart Wright, cartographers at Lonely Planet.

Contributing Photographers

Many of the photographs in this book were taken by Tammy Peluso. Her images have appeared in hundreds of books, brochures, calendars and periodicals. In 1997 she moved to Papua New Guinea, where she established Walindi Photo.

Walt Peterson took the majority of photos in this book. Thanks also to photographers Roslyn Bullas, Phillip Colla, Sue Dippold, Molly Fitzgerald, Diane Gedymen, Tom Haight, Kenneth Howard, Marilyn Kazmers, David Levitt, Jerry Martin, Michael McKay, Michael Peterson, Louisa Preston, Tim Rock, Carl Roessler, Ted Rulison, Hiroshi Sato, Walt Stearns & Bill Warburton

From the Publisher

This first edition was produced in Lonely Planet's U.S. office under direction from Roslyn Bullas, Pisces Books publishing manager. Debra Miller edited this book and Henia Miedzinski designed the book and cover. Scott Summers added production wisdom and support. Senior cartographer Alex Guilbert and Bart Wright created the maps, which were adapted from the author's comprehensive base maps. Thanks to Jean Pierce for contributing text to the Diving Health & Safety section and special thanks to Walt Peterson for his enthusiasm, meticulous research and infinite patience.

Lonely Planet Pisces Books

Lonely Planet acquired the Pisces line of diving and snorkeling books in 1997. The series is being developed and substantially revamped over the next few years. We invite your comments and suggestions.

Pisces Pre-Dive Safety Guidelines

Before embarking on a scuba diving, skin diving or snorkeling trip, careful consideration should be given to the following to ensure a safe and enjoyable experience:

- Possess a current diving certification card from a recognized scuba diving instructional agency (if scuba diving)
- Be sure you are healthy and feel comfortable diving
- Obtain reliable information about physical and environmental conditions at the dive site (e.g. from a reputable local dive operation)
- Be aware of local laws, regulations, and etiquette about marine life and environment
- Dive at sites within your experience level; if available, engage the services of a competent, professionally trained dive instructor or dive master

Underwater conditions vary significantly from one region, or even site, to another. Seasonal changes can significantly alter dive conditions. These differences influence the way divers dress for a dive and what diving techniques they use.

Regardless of location, there are special requirements for diving in that area. Before your dive, ask about the environmental characteristics that can affect your diving and how local, trained divers deal with these considerations.

Warning & Request

Even with dive guides, things change – dive site conditions, regulations, topside information. Nothing stays the same for long. Your feedback on this book will be used to help update future editions and help make the next edition more useful. Excerpts from your correspondence may appear in our newsletter, Planet Talk, or in the Postcards section of our website, so please let us know if you don't want your letter published or your name acknowledged.

Correspondence can be addressed to:
Lonely Planet Publications
Pisces Books
150 Linden Street
Oakland, CA 94607
e-mail: pisces@lonelyplanet.com

Introduction

TAMMY PELUSO

The rugged 1,000 mile– (1,609 km–) long peninsula hanging down like a tail from the U.S. state of California has long enjoyed a reputation for mystery and adventure. Early travelers used colorful phrases to describe it such as, "the tail end of an earthquake," "the land that God forgot," and "a dried stick from the bough of California." In recent years the negative connotations have subsided and the peninsula is now referred to as "Baja California," or simply, "Baja."

Because of its peculiar geography and its part-temperate, part-tropical climate, the waters along Baja's Pacific and Sea of Cortez coasts provide a wide variety of underwater conditions. In a single trip to Baja, divers and snorkelers can explore a cool-water Pacific environment where abalone cling to rocks, cabezon and lingcod swim in kelp forests; a day or two later, they can view such Indo-Pacific beauties as longnose butterflyfish and exotic Moorish idols, both species at home in the warm waters of the coral reef. For the adventurous, the remote and almost unspoiled Islas de Revillagigedo (often called

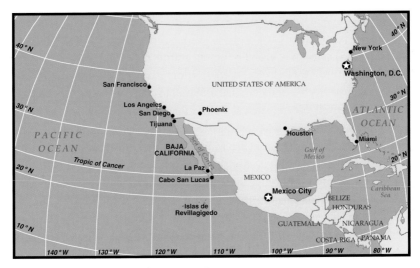

HIROSHI SATO

California sea lions cavort at Los Islotes in the Southern Cortez region.

"the Socorros"), lying several hundred miles south of the peninsula, provide some of the world's best opportunities for seeing large pelagic fish, especially Pacific manta rays and sharks.

Six regions are described in this book: Northern Pacific; Southern Pacific; Northern Cortez; Southern Cortez; the Cape; and the Islas de Revillagigedo. When individual dive sites are clustered within a region, that region is further broken down into areas. Fifty three of Baja's best sites are described in terms of visibility, depth, bottom conditions and expected water temperature. You'll also get specific information on the presence of wrecks, walls, caves, reefs and the marine life you can expect to encounter. Some locations are well known, such as Pulmo Reef, El Bajo Seamount, and Islas los Coronados; others are so remote they may be unknown to all but a few, such as Ánimas Sur and San Pedro Mártir. Detailed information on how to get to the sites is provided, along with contact information for the nearest dive operation. Although the book is not intended as a stand-alone travel guide, the "Baja Practicalities" section gives you some basic topside information, while the "Overview" and "History" sections provide a glimpse into Baja's unique history and cultural heritage. The "Marine Life" section offers a colorful look at some of Baja's most interesting underwater critters.

Overview of Baja

COURTESY OF NASA

Geography

Today's Baja California was firmly attached to
what is now mainland Mexico until about five
million years ago, when the Pacific Plate (includ-
ing Baja and all land west of the San Andreas Fault), began moving to the
northwest. Today the peninsula is one of the most striking geological features
on Earth. Baja's averages less than 70 miles (113 km) in width along its 798-
mile (1,284-km) length, the narrowest part being 26 miles (42 km) from the
Pacific to the western shore of the bay near La Paz, and the greatest being 144
miles (232 km) at the latitude of Punta Eugenia. The shoreline on both coasts
totals 1,980 miles (3,186 km), excluding large, enclosed bays.

MICHAEL McKAY

Secluded bays and beaches, such as this one in Bahía de los Ángeles, provide virtually
unlimited opportunities for independent diving and snorkeling excursions.

11

There are seven principal mountain ranges in Baja. The Sierra de Juárez and the Sierra San Pedro Mártir extend south about 160 miles (258 km) from the border. Baja's highest mountain, a massive double peak named Picacho del Diablo (Devil's Peak), rises to 10,154 ft (3,095 meters). A broken series of mountain ranges runs south from the Sierra San Pedro Mártir, including the Sierra San Borja, the Sierra de San Francisco, the Sierra de Guadalupe and the Sierra de la Giganta, ending north of La Paz. The central part of the Cape region south of La Paz is occupied by the Sierra de la Laguna.

Except for the Río Colorado, now reduced to a relative trickle by dams, only about a half-dozen small streams flow into the Cortez on a more-or-less permanent basis. The so-called Río Mulegé is in fact not a river, but a brackish arm of the Cortez that would become a stagnant swamp without the flushing of the tides. There are only two sizable lakes in Baja. Laguna Salada, in the lowlands south of Mexicali, varies greatly in size from year to year due the changing flows of the Colorado. Laguna Hanson in the Sierra de Juárez is less than a mile across and is shallow and muddy.

There are a number of islands along the peninsula's Pacific coast including Islas los Coronados, Islas de Todos Santos and Islas San Benito, all of great interest to divers and snorkelers. The land animal and plant communities of these islands have been damaged by human activity—goats introduced long ago still ravage plant life, and colonies of nesting sea birds are much smaller than in the past, due to the introduction of rats and cats. Although there is heavy commercial diving and fishing, the marine plants and animals surrounding the islands are fairly intact.

Fishing camps are common along much of Baja's coastline.

About 100 islands and islets dot the Cortez, including Tiburón—the largest—Guardian Angel, San José and Cerralvo. Fresh water is found only on the largest islands and then only in very small amounts. Other than fish, seabird eggs, salt, guano and gypsum, the islands have little direct economic value, which has left plant and animal communities virtually intact. The Cortez islands are now recognized as a treasure of genetic diversity and scientific interest. In 1978, all Cortez islands were granted wildlife-refuge status.

Just south of the U.S./Mexico border are the large, modern cities of Tijuana, Tecate and Mexicali. Farther south, the smaller cities of Ensenada and San Felipe are followed by a series of small towns scattered along the Transpeninsular Highway, the only paved road running the length of the peninsula. South of tiny El Rosario, the cities are left behind and the "real" Baja of lore and legend begins.

Unfenced ranges, lonely ranches, and mile after mile of almost uninhabited desert are broken only by tiny settlements and a few small towns. Just south of the 28th parallel, the sizable town of Guerrero Negro offers the first supermarket south of El Rosario, marking what seems like a return to civilization. The Transpeninsular then turns east toward the Sea of Cortez, passing unique towns such as San Ignacio, a green oasis in a sea of brown like an artifact from a previous century. The road then comes upon Santa Rosalía, once a major copper producer served by a large fleet of sailing ships and steamers from around the world. Turning south along the shores of the Cortez, the highway passes Mulegé, a tropical paradise with its palms and thatched roofs, followed by the bustling town of Loreto. The highway then turns inland to Ciudad Constitución, where vast fields of grain and produce are fed by fossil water from deep wells. Turning southeast, the highway passes La Paz, the capital of the state of Baja California Sur, and then south to San José del Cabo—perhaps the most beautiful town in Baja. Rapidly growing Cabo San Lucas, its harbor filled with yachts from around the world, marks the southern end of the peninsula.

Climate & Oceanography

Most people think of Baja as hot, dry and "tropical." It can indeed get hot—the average summer temperature in Mexicali is 104°-108°F (40°-42°C), with extreme highs reaching 120°F (49°C), making it the hottest place on the continent. And it can be dry—rainfall is extremely low between El Rosario and La Paz, averaging as little as 2-4 inches (5-10 cm) a year, or sometimes only traces for years at a time. A part of the peninsula is in fact tropical: In a 1,057 mile- (1,701 km-) dash down the Transpeninsular Highway, from the border to Cabo San Lucas, you will be south of the Tropic of Cancer for the last 50 miles (81 km).

Baja does get very cold! Water jugs can freeze solid overnight at Picacho del Diablo. The higher reaches of the Sierra de Juárez and Sierra San Pedro Mártir get enough rain to support sizable forests, and micro-climates in the Sierra de la Laguna receive up to 30 inches (76 cm) a year.

The Sea of Cortez experiences some of the world's greatest oceanographic extremes. Its long, narrow configuration produces one of the largest tidal ranges in the world. At the northern end of the Cortez for example, the extreme tidal range—the difference in height between the highest high tide and the lowest low tide each year—is 31 ft (9 meters).

TAMMY PELUSO

Baja's desert vegetation can be surprisingly varied.

Over millions of years, erosion carried by the Colorado River from the Grand Canyon and surrounding lands has deposited on the north end of the Cortez. Low tides uncover mud flats up to 3 miles (5 km) wide. The Cortez used to be far longer than it is now, but over time accumulated silt formed a delta, shortening the Cortez and lengthening the Colorado River. Because little fresh water is transported into the Cortez by rain, rivers and streams, and because evaporation is so great, the Cortez is more saline than the Pacific Ocean.

Surface water temperatures range between 57°F (14°C) and 78°F (26°C) along Baja's Pacific coast. In keeping with its reputation for extremes, water temperatures in the Cortez can reach 91°F (33°C) in the south during summer, but can plummet to 57°F (14°C) in the north during winter.

History

Early Mexico Over the millenniums, a low tundra formation has arisen a number of times in the narrow Bering Strait and nomadic hunters arrived in the New World by simply walking east from the Old. By the arrival of Columbus in 1492, sizable populations were scattered over much of North and South America. One civilization, the Aztecs (or the "Mexica" as they called themselves), dominated neighboring tribes from their center of power located at Tenochtitlan, today's Mexico City. The Aztecs attracted the attention of the Spaniard Hernán Cortés, who assembled a tiny band of adventurers and, between 1519 and 1521, attacked the Aztecs, looting their capital and killing their vacillating, superstition-ridden leader, Montezuma.

The following years were bad for the inhabitants of what is now Mexico, as smallpox (introduced by the Europeans), famine, and conflict greatly reduced their numbers. Scholars disagree wildly in "before" and "after" estimates of the population, but there is general agreement that its decline was one of the greatest demographic disasters in history.

Slowly, however, the situation stabilized. Most of Cortés' army remained in Mexico and, along with additional immigrants from Europe, intermarried with the Indians. Many Indians adopted aspects of European culture, such as the Spanish language, music and religion, while the Europeans took up Indian arts, crafts and foods. As the years passed, a unique culture developed and people began to think of themselves as Mexicans. Mexico achieved its independence from Spain in 1821.

Baja California When the first Europeans visited the peninsula in late 1533 or early 1534, the population was estimated between 30,000 and 50,000. In 1697, the Jesuits began constructing a series of missions, but disease soon took its toll and, due to the increasing lack of souls to save, the missions were abandoned. By by 1767, the Indian population had dropped to perhaps 7,000. Only a few small Indian groups still exist in scattered locations.

Today, the peninsula has a population of over 3.5 million, the vast majority of whom live in Tijuana and Mexicali. The peninsula is divided into two Mexican

The golden altar at the old mission church at San Ignacio.

WALT PETERSON

states: Baja California in the northern half of the peninsula and Baja California Sur in the south. Their capitals are Mexicali and La Paz, respectively. The two states meet at the 28th parallel, just north of Guerrero Negro. In this book, to differentiate between the peninsula and the state, Baja California (the state) is referred to as Baja California [Norte].

Underwater History The wonders of the underwater regions surrounding Baja have long been known. Before the arrival of Europeans, the Seri, Pericú, Cochimí and Guayacura Indians gathered shellfish and speared turtles in shallow waters.

In 1533 or 1534, Hernán Cortés sent two ships to explore the west coast. The crew of one ship mutinied and sailed into a large bay, now known as Bahía de La Paz. Most were killed by the local Indians. However, the few survivors told stories of endless pearls, which later adventurers found to be true, and a thriving industry was established. Since the work was dangerous and exhausting, Indian divers were employed, free-diving without such conveniences as fins, masks and snorkels.

When shallow-water pearl oysters became scarce, hard-hat diving was introduced, but by 1884 the pearl industry began to decline. An oyster farm was established on Isla Espíritu Santo in the early 1900s, the stone and concrete basins of which are still visible. The attempt to farm was too late, however, and the pearl oyster industry ended in 1940, when a blight killed most of the remaining oysters. Still, commercial divers continued to take abalone, clams and scallops and, in recent years, sea urchins and sea cucumbers have been pursued for the restaurants and kitchen tables of Japan.

With the commercial availability of scuba equipment in the late 1940s, small numbers of sport divers began to visit Baja, returning home with glowing tales of underwater adventures. Due to difficult access to dive sites, absence of dive shops and dive travel companies, to say nothing of the unavailability of compressed air, the number of sport divers increased slowly.

Until 1973, no paved roads connected the northern and southern ends of the peninsula. Visitors had few choices concerning transportation: drive to mainland México and take a ferry to La Paz, fly by private plane or commercial airliner, sail by yacht, or risk the grueling unpaved roads in a four-wheel-drive. All that changed with the completion of the Transpeninsular Highway in 1973, opening the peninsula to at least somewhat routine travel. Sport diving and snorkeling expanded and by the late 1980s, they were blossoming. New airports, hotels, launch ramps and marinas enabled more people to make diving trips to the peninsula and new dive operations began to appear. Diving is now a booming industry in Baja, with over 30 dive companies in business on the peninsula. Things have definitely changed since 1533.

Baja Practicalities

Seasons

There are definite seasonal aspects to Baja diving and snorkeling. Summer is the high season as the number of pelagics is at its peak. The reefs are alive with colorful fish courting and then guarding their eggs. Summer also marks the beginning of the *chubasco* season, as well as the occasional *cordonazo*, however tranquil weather is the norm.

September, October and November are the "undiscovered" months for underwater exploration in Baja. The weather cools down, but the water is still warm, the days long and winter winds still at bay. Whale sharks, Manta rays and schools of hammerheads linger along with many other species soon to disappear in the winter months.

In December, January and February air temperatures moderate, making traveling, dining and sleeping pleasant but days short. Occasional cold fronts cause wipe-out conditions along the Pacific coast and heavy winds can cover the Cortez with whitecaps. The cooler water temperature also slows the profusion of marine life.

Weather Wonders

Chubascos (tropical hurricanes) form far south and affect the southern peninsula and surrounding waters from mid-May to mid-November, usually peaking in August and September. The *cordonazo* is a short but severe storm encountered in the summer months during periods of persistent southerly winds. A breeze known as the *coromuel* blows from the south around La Paz almost every day between late spring and early fall, starting in the afternoon until the next morning, bringing welcome relief from the heat of the day.

March, April and May bring warmer air and less wind, but since water temperatures tend to lag behind air temperatures, the water remains relatively cool until mid-April. By May, migratory fish begin to appear, along with more and more eager divers.

La Paz

PLACES TO STAY
19 Los Arcos Hotel
27 Aquamarine RV Park

PLACES TO EAT
1 Restaurant Adriana
4 Restaurant Kiwi
8 Carlos 'n Charlie's
16 Restaurant Bismark

OTHER
2 Aero México
3 Tourism Office
5 Post Office
6 PEMEX Station
7 Museo de Anthropologia
9 Baja Outdoor Activities
11 Bank
12 Customs Office
15 Aero California Office
17 Laundromat
18 PEMEX Station
20 Hertz Car Rental
21 Hospital
23 Avis Car Rental
24 Marina de La Paz
25 Agencia Arjona
   (marine supplies)
26 Mercury/Mariner Outboar
28 PEMEX Station
30 PEMEX Station
31 Baja California Motors
32 Bus Terminal

DIVE OPERATIONS
10 Baja Diving & Service
13 Scuba Baja Joe
14 Scu-Baja Dive Center
22 Centro de Buceo Carey
27 La Paz Diving Service
29 Baja Expeditions

Cabo San Lucas

PLACES TO STAY
1 El Faro Viejo Trailer Park
4 Club Cascades de Baja
11 Meliá San Lucas
22 Marina Fiesta Resort
24 Hotel Mar de Cortez
28 Hotel Hacienda
32 Hotel Plaza las Glorias
35 Terra Sol Beach Resort
36 Hotel Finisterra
40 Hotel Solmar

PLACES TO EAT
8 Peacock's
9 Edith's
11 Jennifer's
12 Las Palmas Lobster Hous
16 El Squid Roe
25 Cabo Wabo
26 Giggling Marlin
27 Carlos 'n Charlie's
30 Fisherman's Pescadores
37 El Galeón

OTHER
2 PEMEX Station
3 Immigration Office
6 Dollar Car Rental
7 Post Office
14 Bus Station
15 Thrifty Car Rental
18 Marina Cabo San Lucas
19 Captain of the Port
20 El Pescadería el Dorado
21 Marina Launch Ramp
23 Bank
29 Customs Office
31 Plaza Nautica
33 Fuel Dock
34 US Consular Agency
38 Open Air Market

DIVE OPERATIONS
13 Tío Sports
17 Plaza Bonita Mall:
   J&R Baja Divers
32 Plaza las Glorias:
   Baja Dive Expeditions,
   Land's End Divers,
   Neptune Divers,
   Pacific Coast Adventures,
   Underwater Diversions
39 Amigos del Mar

RECOMPRESSION CHAMBERS
5 Dr Alfonso Nájar Clinic
32 Buseo Medico Mexicano

Getting There

International airports are located at Tijuana, Mexicali, Loreto, La Paz and San José del Cabo. A ferry system operates between Santa Rosalía and Guaymas, between La Paz and Topolobampo, and La Paz and Mazatlán. You can get information on buses and ferries from the offices of the State Secretary of Tourism, for both California [Norte] and California Sur. For contact information, see the Listings section at the back of the book.

If you plan to drive, you must have a valid, original registration or a notarized bill of sale for all private vehicles, driven, towed, or carried; the same goes for trailers and boats. Bring the original and two copies. If there is a lien on any of these, or if any are borrowed, you must have a notarized letter from the lienholder or owner authorizing you to take it into Mexico.

Drivers should obtain vehicle insurance. Policies for one day or more are available at many insurance offices near all U.S. border crossings and some have drive-up services open 24 hours a day. All insurance companies offer discounts for long policies and most accept VISA, MasterCard and American Express. The best insurance rates are offered by the **Discover Baja Travel Club** and the **Vagabundos del Mar Boat and Travel Club**. If you are towing a trailer, it must be insured along with the tow vehicle.

If you plan to travel with your vehicle to mainland Mexico, contact a Mexican Consulate or Tourism Office and obtain a copy of *Traveling to Mexico by Car*, published by the Secretary of Tourism. This booklet describes the procedures required upon entrance and departure. If you are bringing a boat, you may need a boat permit, so contact the Mexico Ministry of the Environment, Natural Resources and Fisheries for current requirements.

Los Ángeles Verdes

"The Green Angels" consist of a fleet of green pickup trucks, each normally crewed by two men, hopefully somewhat proficient in English. They can assist with minor repairs, provide small parts, sell gas and oil at cost and arrange for towing and repairs. Most highways are patrolled once a day, occasionally less often. The trucks are equipped with CB radios, a few with short-wave.

The Green Angels have an honored history and their services have not been limited to strictly mechanical matters. In recent years, they used a piece of clear plastic and some duct tape to patch a motor home windshield when a rock thrown up by a passing 18-wheeler punched a hole through it; dealt with assorted rattlesnake bites and scorpion stings; and helped a mother convince a tearful little girl that the caracaras and vultures perched on the cacti around their scalloping camp at the south end of Bahía Concepción really don't carry children away. Even if you never need their services, it's great to know that *Los Ángeles Verdes* are around.

The Transpeninsular Highway

The only paved road extending the length of the peninsula, the two-lane Transpeninsular Highway (Route 1) is narrower than its U.S. counterparts.

WALT PETERSON

Shoulders are thin or nonexistent and striping and safety signs are often absent. Much of the land along the highway is unfenced rangeland and cattle, burros and goats wander onto the highway at night, drawn to the heat of the road. Thus the two basic safety rules on the Transpeninsular are: don't speed and don't drive at night.

Petroleum products in Mexico are sold by PEMEX, an inefficient government monopoly. Stations rarely offer more than gas and oil and a small selection of filters, additives, fan belts and minor parts. If you are lucky enough to find an operational rest room bring your own toilet paper. PEMEX does not take credit cards, so payment must

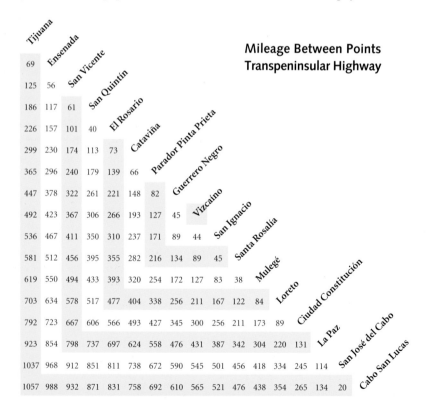

**Mileage Between Points
Transpeninsular Highway**

Tijuana	Ensenada	San Vicente	San Quintín	El Rosario	Cataviña	Parador Pinta Prieta	Guerrero Negro	Vizcaíno	San Ignacio	Santa Rosalía	Mulegé	Loreto	Ciudad Constitución	La Paz	San José del Cabo	Cabo San Lucas
69																
125	56															
186	117	61														
226	157	101	40													
299	230	174	113	73												
365	296	240	179	139	66											
447	378	322	261	221	148	82										
492	423	367	306	266	193	127	45									
536	467	411	350	310	237	171	89	44								
581	512	456	395	355	282	216	134	89	45							
619	550	494	433	393	320	254	172	127	83	38						
703	634	578	517	477	404	338	256	211	167	122	84					
792	723	667	606	566	493	427	345	300	256	211	173	89				
923	854	798	737	697	624	558	476	431	387	342	304	220	131			
1037	968	912	851	811	738	672	590	545	501	456	418	334	245	114		
1057	988	932	871	831	758	692	610	565	521	476	438	354	265	134	20	

be in cash. Stations are rarely open all night and they offer no mechanical services—if you need a mechanic you find a *mechánico*. Gasoline comes in two grades, Magnasin and Premium. Diesel can be easier to find than in the U.S. Gas prices are comparable with U.S. prices. Do not depend on finding gasoline at every station along the Transpeninsular, especially on long holidays and during winter. The PEMEX stations at Cataviña, Parador Punta Prieta and Villa Jesús María are often out of gas or closed. The basic rule for drivers in this notorious "gas gap" is to top off before your tank is half-empty. Kilometer (KM) signs are marked along the Transpeninsular. In the driving directions in this book, a "+" after the KM number means the site occurs about half-way between that marker and the next highest marker.

Getting Around

If you fly in on a package trip, you should have little trouble getting to your destination; many hotels have shuttles that will pick you up at the airport. If not, mini-van service often runs between the airports and major hotels. Taxis are available in all large cities and in some of the smaller ones, such as Loreto. Should you wish to do some sightseeing or exploring, all the international airports have vehicle rental desks and most tourist hotels have an agency in the lobby or can otherwise arrange rentals. Make sure you get insurance and understand the limitations put on rental vehicles—most rental companies prohibit off-road driving.

Several bus lines offer inexpensive transportation between the towns along the Transpeninsular and other highways, but divers with full gear are likely to find this to be untenable, despite the low cost. If you are tempted, information on routes, schedules and costs can be obtained from the State Secretary of Tourism offices.

Immigration

U.S. citizens must have a Tourist Card in order to stay more than 72 hours in border areas, or to travel south of Maneadero or San Felipe. Cards can be obtained at Mexican Government Tourism Offices, consulates and embassies, some airlines, insurance companies, travel agencies and from all Mexican Immigration offices. You must show proof of citizenship, such as a valid passport or certified birth certificate. Tourist Cards must be used within 90 days of issue and the document used to prove citizenship must also be carried while you are in Mexico. A person under 18 traveling without both parents present must have a notarized letter granting permission to travel in Mexico.

These requirements apply to Canadians as well. If you are neither a U.S. or Canadian citizen or a legal resident of the U.S. or Canada, inquire at a Mexican Consulate or Mexican Government Tourism Office for current entry requirements.

Time

The state of Baja California [Norte], occupying the peninsula from the U.S. border to the 28th parallel of latitude (near Guerrero Negro), uses Pacific Standard Time (PST). The state of Baja California Sur to the south, with stronger ties to mainland Mexico, uses Mountain Standard Time (MST), which is one hour earlier. PST is eight hours behind Greenwich Mean Time, MST seven hours.

Electricity

Baja California uses the same 110-volt, 60-cycle system used in the U.S. and Canada. However, if you plan to bring any appliances or equipment that require grounded outlets (three-prong), be sure to bring along a 3-2 adapter, available in any hardware store.

Weights & Measures

Mexico uses the metric system; distance is measured in kilometers, weight in kilograms, length in meters and centimeters, volume in liters and temperature in degrees Celsius. Both metric and imperial measurements are given in this book, except for specific driving instructions, which are provided in miles. General dive site descriptions are given in both feet and meters, however more specific depth information is provided in feet. See the conversion chart at the back of the book for equivalents.

What to Bring

Divers and snorkelers will encounter a greater range of water temperatures in the Cortez and along Baja's Pacific coast than they have probably experienced anywhere else. You'll require everything from a full 7mm wetsuit to a 2mm shorty, and possibly just a Lycra skin. Few dive operations rent wetsuits, so plan to bring your own. A few dive operations rent dive lights, DIN adapters for European equipment and dive computers with air-integration; most rent tanks, BCs, regulators, weight belts, masks, snorkels

WALT PETERSON

A Cortez free-diver suits up before a dive.

and fins. Other than those in the Cape region, few operations sell much in the way of equipment. Tanks need to be recently tested before any dive operation on the peninsula will fill them. No dive operation on the peninsula will pump out-of-hydro tanks (tanks that have not undergone a hydrostatic test in the past five years).

Divers and snorkelers planning a foray to any location in the Northern Cortez region should obtain and use a set of tide tables as a central part of planning for the trip, something no less important than a road map. *Tide Tables for the West Coast of North and South America* is published by the National Oceanic and Atmospheric Administration. NOAA has tidal stations at Ensenada, San Carlos, La Paz, at the entrance to the Colorado River and on the eastern shores of the Cortez. The University of Arizona publishes tables for the northern Cortez.

Your topside wardrobe will depend on when and where you go. Year round, bring clothes appropriate for warm, dry, sunny weather, including short- and long-sleeved shirts, shorts and long pants. Wear light, reflective colors (you will be cooler) and bring a wide-brimmed hat. A windbreaker may be needed in fall and spring, especially along Pacific shores. During winter, it can get downright cold and you should have a coat and a sweater or pullover.

Certain things should be left home. Being apprehended with more than a token amount of marijuana, cocaine and other illicit substances will result in a minimum jail sentence of 10 years. Even a small amount will result in deportation. If you drive in Baja you will encounter military check points and your vehicle is subject to search, even without probable cause. If you have a medical condition that requires narcotics such as Percodan,

Percoset, or codeine, keep them in their prescription containers. Do not bring firearms, Mace, or pepper spray.

Don't forget your diving certification card. All Baja dive operations require them for equipment sales and rentals. Yours was lost or left behind? Some operations will attempt to confirm certification by telephone, but if this fails, you may have to take a resort course. No operations firmly demand log books.

Underwater Photography & Video

Subjects for underwater photography and video range in size from huge whale sharks down to tiny nudibranchs, and visibility ranges from 100 ft (30 meters) down to just a few, so prudent photographers should bring a range of equipment, including wide-angle lenses, extension rings and framers. Buy all the film you need before leaving home. C-41-process color print film in 100-, 200- and 400-speed by Fuji, Konica and Kodak is available in the larger towns, but is expensive and color transparency film is very difficult to find. Video film is available only in the larger towns and camcorder batteries will

Look, take a photo, but don't touch—the stone scorpionfish's spines can cause nasty wounds.

prove elusive everywhere. Common AA and D batteries are available, but don't expect to find button batteries for a Nikonos. Processing for C-41 film is available in the larger towns, but long, deep scratches and distorted colors are common, so wait until you get home to get your processing done.

The greatest challenge to underwater photographers in Baja is combating dust, which is hard to avoid if you're traveling by road. Bring along a supply of large Ziplock bags to store cameras, equipment and film (also handy for Walkmans, audio tapes and CDs).

In Cabo San Lucas, **Pacific Coast Adventures** offers rental housings for disposable cameras, **Underwater Diversions** has an Underwater Photographer course and **J & R Divers** will prepare professional video production. Some of the dive boats provide camera dips so you can rinse off your camera gear.

Money

U.S. dollars are accepted almost everywhere in Baja, but convert at least some of your money to pesos and use it to pay for all cash transactions. Since virtually all businesses make change in pesos, you will soon be dealing with a confusing mix of dollars and pesos whether you like it or not. Conversion rates at airports, hotels, restaurants, border crossings and other businesses are usually unfavorable. The peso fluctuates dramatically, so don't convert large amounts or plan to hold pesos for long periods. Many businesses and gas stations can't make change for large peso notes, so get your pesos in small denominations.

Many businesses catering to tourists accept major credit cards, but don't plan to use them in smaller towns or at businesses used by the local people. Using personal checks in Baja ranges from difficult to impossible. Many banks have automatic teller machines (ATMs), but if you do not wish to use them, buy small-denomination traveler's checks before you leave.

Business Hours

Business hours are generally from 9 am to 2 pm and from 4 pm to 7 pm weekdays. What happens in the two missing hours? It is the traditional *siesta* time. However, in touristy areas, *siesta* is largely a thing of the past. Banks are usually open from 9 am to 1:30 pm. There are numerous legal holidays and many towns and cities have civic holidays—check with the office of the appropriate State Secretary of Tourism.

Accommodations

Hotel accommodations in Baja run the gamut from absolutely no-frills to absolutely luxurious. The best are generally less expensive than their counterparts in the U.S., Canada and Europe and the cheapest rooms may cost as little as $15/night. Some of the better hotels are affiliated with chains in the U.S., such as Best Western. The La Pinta chain operates hotels in San Quintín, Cataviña, Guerrero Negro, San Ignacio and Loreto. They are beautiful and have good restaurants, but the fare is a bit steep, at least by Baja standards.

The pool at the Solmar Hotel
in Cabo San Lucas.

The proprietors of Baja's motels have an aversion to the term "motel," and choose the grander "hotel." The hotels along the Transpeninsular cater primarily to the locals. Most are rather utilitarian, but they are priced appropriately. Many people enjoy simply spending the night at a remote beach, which costs nothing.

See the Listings section for information on establishments catering primarily to divers and snorkelers. Information on other hotels, motels and RV parks can be obtained from the State Secretary of Tourism of Baja California [Norte] and that for the state of Baja California Sur, as well as Discover Baja and the Vagabundos.

Dining & Food

Restaurant meals vary widely in price, depending on the season, the establishment and the food you order. If you choose restaurants at resorts and tourist hotels or fancy restaurants in the large cities and towns, you will pay about what you would in an equivalent establishment in the U.S. or Canada. Restaurant cuisine includes Argentine, Austrian, Basque, Chinese, French, German, Italian, Japanese, Moroccan, American, International, Continental, and even Mexican. There is no particularly "Baja" cuisine, but fresh-catch fish dinners can be superb, with excellent seasoning and often lots of garlic.

Grocery stores range from humble, one-room adobe shacks in the smaller settlements to supermarkets in the larger towns. If you are preparing your own meals, you can save considerable amounts of money if you buy Mexican-made products used by the locals.

Things to Buy

In touristy areas, shops and stalls sell a great variety of products, especially clothing, colorful paper mâché animals, curios, figurines, *huaraches* (leather sandals), ironwood carvings, jewelry, leather work, pottery, ceramics and glassware and *serapes* (brightly colored, blanket-like shawls). Baja may well be the T-shirt capital of the world, and some of the shops seem to be in competition to see who can sell the raunchiest. Except for the high-end clothing and jewelry stores, prices are fluid and bargaining is expected.

Common items offered for sale in Baja that are illegal to import into the U.S. include Cuban cigars, sea-turtle products such as jewelry, cosmetics containing turtle shell or oil, whale bones, teeth and baleen, wildlife curios such as stuffed iguanas, some species of cacti, and virtually all live birds. All jewelry made from black coral is prohibited.

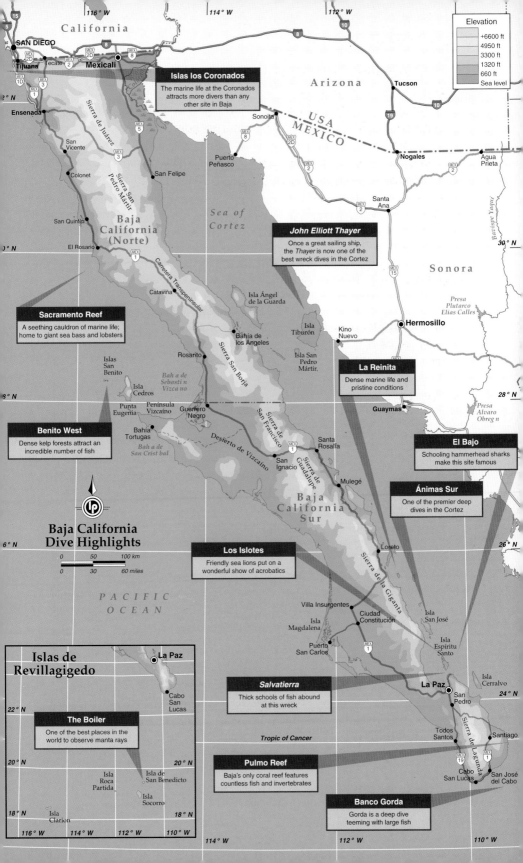

Baja California Dive Highlights

Islas los Coronados
The marine life at the Coronados attracts more divers than any other site in Baja

John Elliott Thayer
Once a great sailing ship, the *Thayer* is now one of the best wreck dives in the Cortez

Sacramento Reef
A seething cauldron of marine life; home to giant sea bass and lobsters

La Reinita
Dense marine life and pristine conditions

Benito West
Dense kelp forests attract an incredible number of fish

El Bajo
Schooling hammerhead sharks make this site famous

Ánimas Sur
One of the premier deep dives in the Cortez

Los Islotes
Friendly sea lions put on a wonderful show of acrobatics

Salvatierra
Thick schools of fish abound at this wreck

Pulmo Reef
Baja's only coral reef features countless fish and invertebrates

Banco Gorda
Gorda is a deep dive teeming with large fish

Islas de Revillagigedo

The Boiler
One of the best places in the world to observe manta rays

Elevation

	+6600 ft
	4950 ft
	3300 ft
	1320 ft
	660 ft
	Sea level

Scale

| 0 | 50 | 100 km |
| 0 | 30 | 60 miles |

Activities & Attractions

WALT PETERSON

Parque Nacional San Pedro Mártir

High in the mountains to the east of Colonet is a wonderful but little-used national park, the finest in Baja. A trip to the park will radically realign of your image of the peninsula. Despite Baja's stereotype as hot, dry, and tropical, the park has trees such as Coulter, Jeffrey, lodgepole and sugar pine, incense cedar, white fir and quaking aspen. The rare San Pedro Mártir cypress is found in a few isolated areas, with the largest known individual having a circumference of 15 ft (5 meters). There are open meadows, year-round creeks and even trout streams. To get to the park, drive to KM 140+, 87 miles (140 km) south of Ensenada on the Transpeninsular, and turn east on the graded dirt and gravel road. Set odometer. The entrance to the park is at mile 47.4. Adventures in the park include hiking, backpacking and climbing Picacho Diablo.

WALT PETERSON

Hikers enjoy the pine forest in Parque Nacional San Pedro Mártir on a crisp fall day.

Rock Art

Early Indian tribes graced the peninsula with art treasures ranging from simple petroglyphs pecked on rocks to enormous murals painted on cave walls. Rock art appears at more than a hundred sites in Baja, the most spectacular near the town of San Ignacio. The murals depict figures of humans and animals, painted life size or larger on such a grand scale that local legends insist the artists were giants. Visits to these sites can be arranged by visiting the new museum at San Ignacio. Trips range from day-trips to three-day forays by burro to the crown jewel of Baja rock art, Gardner Cave. Visits to other sites on the peninsula can be made through most tourist hotels from Santa Rosalía south to Los Cabos.

Whale Watching

Early in October, gray whales begin a 5,000-mile (8,047-km) journey from Alaska south to Laguna Guerrero Negro, Scammon's Lagoon, Laguna San Ignacio and Bahía Magdalena. It is the longest migration route of any mammal. About half of the mature females conceived the previous year and are about to give birth. Most others are ready for breeding, many having

A whale encounter at Laguna San Ignacio.

given birth the past year. Approximately 1,500 grays are born each year, about half in Scammon's Lagoon. The return migration to Arctic waters begins in late January, although a few mothers and calves remain as late as May or June. It is estimated that over a million humans catch a glimpse of these whales each year along the western coast of Baja and the U.S., making them the "most-seen" whales in the world. Some of the whales seem just as curious about humans. In a number of locations—especially Laguna San Ignacio—mother whales will come right up to boats, showing off their new offspring. Visits to Laguna San Ignacio can be arranged at the Kuyima Servicios Ecoturisticos office in the town square at San Ignacio. A number of organizations in Guerrero Negro and Puerto Lopéz Mateos offer local trips. Parque Natural de la Ballena Gris is a national park devoted to the whales, access to which can be found at KM 208 off the Transpeninsular, just east of Guerrero Negro.

Big Game Fishing

Baja is home to one of the finest marlin and sailfish areas in the world. The most productive are centered in the Cape region, especially off East Cape and Cabo San Lucas. While some striped marlin and sailfish hang around all year, the best fishing normally occurs between May and October. There are resorts catering mainly to fishermen, and cruisers are readily available for charter. Divers and snorkelers with their own boats, even small inflatables and outboards, have an excellent chance for a striped marlin.

Windsurfing

The number of windsurfers visiting Baja has increased dramatically in recent years—Baja has finally been "discovered," and for good reason, for there is everything anyone could want, ranging from mill ponds to rolling ocean swells, from gentle zephyrs to boom-bending blasts. While there are many good areas along both the Pacific and Cortez coasts, the best conditions and most consistent winds are found at East Cape. A number of resorts cater to windsurfers and most will provide equipment and instruction to "walk-ins" (people not participating in package trips or staying at the resort), subject to first call by guests.

Diving Health & Safety

TAMMY PELUSO

General Health

The two most common health concerns of divers and snorkelers in Baja are Montezuma's revenge (diarrhea) and sunburn. Both can be completely avoided or greatly minimized by following a few simple precautions.

Use only bottled water (readily available throughout the peninsula), for drinking and food preparation and limit the use of local water to washing and flushing. Avoid greasy, highly seasoned and/or unaccustomed foods. Wash, peel and/or cook all fresh food; take care in selecting restaurants and if you buy ice for refrigeration or to cool drinks, look for the words *agua purificada* (purified water) on the plastic bag. If these fail, try Imodium A-D, available in many Baja pharmacies and supermarkets.

Sunblock lotions and lipbalms SPF 15 or higher are essential. Use a waterproof brand if you're in and out of the water and reapply often. Snorkelers should take special care to avoid getting burned on their backs while in the water.

Pre-trip Preparation

A number of full-service dive shops operate in Baja, especially in La Paz and in the Cape region, where you can buy or rent almost anything, but shops elsewhere are generally rather modest. Most can provide basic diving equipment rentals, but generally do not offer much in the way of sales. Even if you are participating in a package trip or staying at a dive resort, conduct a detailed inventory of all your dive equipment so you can make all needed repairs and adjustments before

Diving and Flying

While it's fine to dive soon *after* flying, it's important to remember that your last dive should be completed at least 12 hours (some experts advise 24 hours) *before* your flight to minimize the risk of residual nitrogen in the blood that can cause decompression injury.

you travel. Even the smallest problems—a regulator that frequently goes into free-flow, a BC with an air leak, a badly chafed fin or mask strap, a tank valve missing its O-ring, a loose wetsuit seam—all can become big problems.

Start exercising at least a month before you leave. If you haven't been diving in six months or more, especially if you've logged fewer than 20 dives, take a refresher dive or two, even if it's just in a pool.

Tips for Evaluating a Dive Operator

First impressions mean a lot. Ask yourself a few questions: Does the business appear organized and professionally staffed? Does it prominently display its affiliation with a diving oganization such as NAUI, PADI or SSI? This is generally a good indication that the operation adheres to high standards.

Rental equipment should be well rinsed. If you see sand or salt crystals, watch out. Before starting your dive, inspect the equipment thoroughly: Check the hoses for wear, see that mouthpieces are secure and make sure you've got a depth and air pressure gauge.

After gearing up and turning on your air, listen for air leaks. Now test your BC: push the power inflator to make sure it functions correctly (and doesn't free-flow); if it fails, get another BC—don't try to inflate it manually; make sure the BC holds air. Then purge your regulator a bit and smell the air. It should be odorless. If you detect an oily or otherwise bad odor, try a different tank and then start searching for another operator.

Medical & Recompression Facilities

There are doctors and dentists in all the larger towns and cites and even in some of the smaller villages. Some drugs requiring a prescription elsewhere can be bought over the counter in Baja.

WALT PETERSON

The recompression chamber at Club Hotel Cantamar in La Paz.

Four recompression chambers are operational in Baja. One is off the road to Punta Banda, just south of Ensenada. It is owned by a sea urchin cooperative and is staffed by a doctor. The chamber in La Paz is at the Club Hotel Cantamar, on the road to Pichilingue; information can be obtained by calling Baja Diving & Service. There are two chambers in Cabo San Lucas; Buseo Medico Méxicano is in Plaza Marina; the other is at the clinic of Dr. Alfonso Nájar. The nearest chamber in the U.S. is at Hyperbaric Technology, Inc. in San Diego. Chambers also exist at El Rosario, Isla Cedros, Isla Natividad, San Carlos and Bahía Tortugas. These are owned by the local fishing cooperatives and, except in the most dire emergency, you should not not depend on these chambers.

> ## Recompression Chambers
>
> **Baja Diving & Service**
> 1665 Obregón, La Paz, BCS, México
> ☎ 112-21826 fax: 112-28644
>
> **Buseo Medico Méxicano**
> Plaza Marina E-16, Cabo San Lucas, BCS, México ☎ 114-33666 fax: 114-34088
>
> **Hyperbaric Technology, Inc.**
> 200 W Arbor Drive, San Diego, CA 92103
> ☎ 619-543-5222 (24 hours)
>
> **Dr. Alfonso Nájar**
> Venustiano Carranza 11, e/ Abasolo y Ocampo, Cabo San Lucas, BCS, México
> ☎ 114-31218 Cellular ☎ 114-75919
> Pager: 114-35050, ext. 1501
>
> **Unidad de Tratamiento Hiperbarico Fanavi**
> (sea urchin processing plant)
> Ejido C. Esteban Cantú, KM 10, Carretera La Bufadora, Punta Banda, BC, México
> ☎ 617-16281 (doctor's cellular phone)
> ☎ 615-42050 (sea urchin processing plant)

DAN

Divers Alert Network (DAN) is an international membership association of individuals and organizations sharing a common interest in diving and safety. It operates a 24-hour diving emergency hotline, ☎ **919-684-8111** or **919-684-4DAN** (919-684-4DAN (-4326) accepts collect calls in a dive emergency). DAN does not directly provide medical care; however, it does provide advice on early treatment, evacuation and hyperbaric treatment of diving-related injuries. Divers should contact DAN for assistance as soon as a diving emergency is suspected. DAN membership is reasonably priced and includes DAN TravelAssist, a membership benefit, which covers medical air evacuation from anywhere in the world for any illness or injury. DAN members are also eligible for secondary dive accident insurance coverage. For membership questions call ☎ 800-446-2671 in the U.S. or ☎ 919-684-2948 elsewhere.

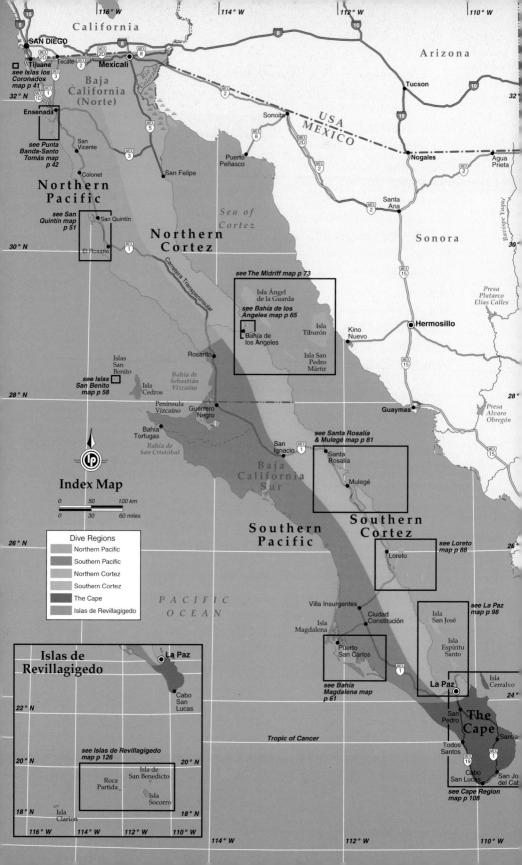

Diving in Baja California

WALT PETERSON

Diving is booming in Baja, with over 30 dive operations and a number of live-aboard dive boats. Most of Baja's dive sites are boat dives and the best sites lie in the Southern Cortez and Cape regions, or even farther south at the Revilligigedos. The number of good beach dives, at least those in reasonably accessible locations, is limited—of the 53 sites described in this book, only 8 are beach dives.

For the purposes of this book, the waters surrounding Baja have been broken down into areas within six regions: the Northern Pacific, the Southern Pacific, the Northern Cortez, the Southern Cortez, the Cape, and the Islas de Revillagigedo. This chapter takes the reader down Baja's Pacific coast, up again to the north end of the Cortez, south to Cabo San Lucas and ending at the Revillagigedos. The dive site descriptions illustrate the dramatic changes in underwater conditions and marine life you can experience as you travel through the different regions. Average winter (W) and summer (S) water temperatures are given for each site as well as the typical visibility you can expect in both seasons.

Snorkeling

Snorkelers will find much to enjoy; of the 53 sites described in the book, over 40 have shallow areas, generally good visibility, and dense marine life. Of the five best, four have easy beach access—La Bufadora, Pulmo, Chileno and Santa María—while the fifth, The Aquarium at Isla Socorro, can be reached only by

TAMMY PELUSO

Snorkelers enter the water off a beautiful beach in Los Cabos.

live-aboard. Advanced snorkelers with a taste for adventure may wish to explore deeper waters in hopes of encountering large pelagic fish. The best sites for this activity are Johnston's Seamount, Rocosa, Ánimas Sur, El Bajo, Cerralvo South, Los Frailes, Banco Gorda, The Boiler and Roca O'Neal. All are boat dives except for Los Frailes.

Would-be divers work on certification in a Cabo San Lucas pool.

Certification

The Southern Cortez and Cape regions have much to offer if you wish to pursue certification or take specialty courses: the water is warm, conditions consistent and the weather is usually reliable. The three international airports and easy local ground transportation, hotels and other amenities contribute to make the diving easy and hassle-free. Due to their wealth of marine life, these two regions are ideal for pursuing an underwater naturalist course, especially at Pulmo. With magnificent beaches and many shops, your non-aquatic friends, spouse and children will be kept busy while you take classes. Since it has only two dive operations, neither of which offers instruction, the Northern Pacific region is not well suited for taking certification or specialty courses, and the Southern Pacific region has no dive operations at all.

Pisces Rating System for Dives & Divers

The dive sites in this book are rated according to the following diver skill level rating system. These are not absolute ratings but apply to divers at a particular time, diving at a particular place. For instance, someone unfamiliar with prevailing conditions might be considered a novice diver at one dive area, but an intermediate diver at another, more familiar location.

Novice: A novice diver generally fits the following profile:
◆ basic scuba certification from an internationally recognized certifying agency
◆ dives infrequently (less than one trip a year)
◆ logged fewer than 25 total dives
◆ dives no deeper than 18 meters (60 ft)
◆ little or no experience diving in similar waters and conditions
* A novice diver should be accompanied by an instructor, divemaster or advanced diver on all dives

Intermediate: An intermediate diver generally fits the following profile:
◆ may have participated in some form of continuing diver education
◆ logged between 25 and 100 dives
◆ dives no deeper than 40 meters (130 ft)
◆ has been diving within the last six months in similar waters and conditions

Advanced: An advanced diver generally fits the following profile:
◆ advanced certification
◆ has been diving for more than 2 years; logged over 100 dives
◆ has been diving within the last six months in similar waters and conditions

Regardless of skill level, you should be in good physical condition and know your limitations. If you are uncertain as to which category you fit, ask the advice of a local dive instructor. He or she is best qualified to assess your abilities based on the prevailing dive conditions at any given site. Ultimately you must decide if you are capable of making a particular dive, depending on your level of training, recent experience, and physical condition, as well as water conditions at the site. Remember that water conditions can change at any time, even during a dive.

Dive Site Icons

The symbols at the beginning of the dive site descriptions provide a quick summary of some of the following characteristics present at the site:

 Good snorkeling or free-diving site.

 Remains or partial remains of a shipwreck can be seen at this site.

 The site has a drop-off that may lure divers into depths beyond their skill level.

 The best parts of the dive occur in water deeper than 60 ft (18.3 meters).

 Strong currents may be encountered at this site.

 Strong surge (the horizontal movement of water caused by waves) may be encountered at this site.

 Drift dive. Because of strong currents and/or difficulty in anchoring, a drift dive is recommended at this site.

 The site often has visibility of less than 25 ft.

 Cave will be found at this site. Only experienced cave divers should explore inner cave areas.

 Marine Preserve. Special regulations apply in this area.

Northern Pacific Dive Sites

The Northern Pacific region covers Baja's Pacific coast from Islas los Coronados to just short of Islas San Benito. The cool California Current sets south in this region and the average annual tidal range is about 4.5 ft (1 meter). A trip to the region requires a small investment in time and money, but you'll be rewarded with excellent diving and snorkeling at a number of relatively pristine and uncrowded sites. There are currently only two dive operations in this region, **Almar Dive Shop** and **La Bufadora Dive**.

California divers will feel at home in the Northern Pacific region—the water temperature, weather and marine life are much the same. Among the creatures seen here are black and red abalone, blacksmith, cabezon, calico rockfish, California barracuda, California halibut, California sheephead, California spiny lobster, garibaldi, halfmoon, kelp bass, lingcod, ocean whitefish, opaleye, yellowtail and several species of sea urchin. The vast "forests" of kelp in this region take a beating in El Niño years, but have a history of bouncing back.

LOIS ANN DIVE CHARTERS

The *Lois Ann* dive boat off Isla Coronado del Norte.

California sea lions relax in the sun.

Islas los Coronados Dive Sites

	Good Snorkeling	Novice	Intermediate	Advanced
1a Pukey Point			✓	✓
1b Lobster Shack		✓	✓	✓
1c McDonald's	✓	✓	✓	✓

1 Islas los Coronados

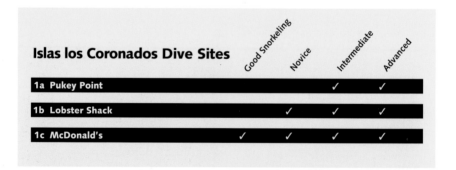

Islas los Coronados consist of two main islands—Coronado del Norte and Coronado del Sur—plus Middle Rock and Middle Island, two small islands located between the two large ones. Coronado del Norte has the better dive sites. Pukey

Access: Boat from San Diego about 1½ hrs

Temperature W/S: 57/62°F (14/17°C)

Visibility W/S: 50/30 ft (15/9 meters)

Point at the north end is spectacular but, as the name implies, it is usually rough and often has strong currents, occasionally a challenge even for experienced divers. Just south of Pukey Point on the eastern side of the island is a tiny cove called Lobster Shack, where thousands of divers have made their first open-water dive. Farther down the island toward the southern tip is McDonald's, which has an arch that you can swim through to the west side of the island on calm days.

Many divers agree that one of the highlights of diving at the Coronados is the interaction with sea lions. Young pups are here from November through March. Curious and fearless, they often mimic whatever the divers do. Sometimes, while divers get ready, groups of sea lions do flips behind the boat, enticing the divers to hurry into the water.

Other Coronodos dive sites include, the Middle Grounds, north of Middle Rock; The Slot, between the two middle islands; and Jack-Ass Rock Ledge, three-quarters of a mile east of the lighthouse on the south tip of Coronado del Sur. A reef extending north from Coronado del Sur has rich sea life, including unusual invertebrates like the chestnut cowrie and the white sea urchin. The northern and western shores of all four islands are exposed to full Pacific swell so few divers explore them, despite their more prolific marine animals and plants. When the Santa Ana wind is blowing however, or when winds and seas are calm, local dive boats visit these areas.

A number of boats from San Diego visit the Coronados for day-trips, including the *Lois Ann* and *Ocean Odyssey*. Private boats can be launched in San Diego.

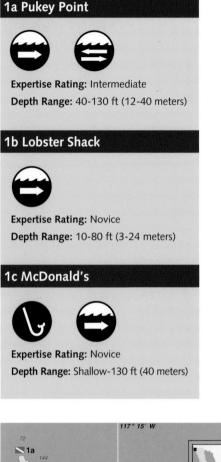

1a Pukey Point

Expertise Rating: Intermediate
Depth Range: 40-130 ft (12-40 meters)

1b Lobster Shack

Expertise Rating: Novice
Depth Range: 10-80 ft (3-24 meters)

1c McDonald's

Expertise Rating: Novice
Depth Range: Shallow-130 ft (40 meters)

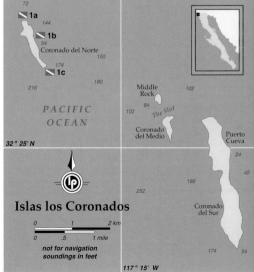

Islas los Coronados

not for navigation
soundings in feet

Punta Banda-Santo Tomás Area

The finest diving and snorkeling near Ensenada is in the Punta Banda–Santo Tomás area, which consists of five dive sites: Kennedy's, La Bufadora, Cabo Banda, Islas de Todos Santos and Rocas Soledad. To get to the first four sites, drive to Maneadero, 8.6 miles south of Ensenada on the Transpeninsular. Turn west on the road to Punta Banda, and set odometer. At mile 6, note the dirt road running south, just east of **Loco Lobo RV Park**. This leads to the **Unidad de Tratamiento Hiperbarico Fanavi** recompression chamber. At mile 7.6 are two RV camps, **La Jolla Beach Camp** and **Villarino Camp**, the first of which has a concrete boat ramp. The turnoff for Kennedy's is found at mile 8. At mile 8.7, a road runs north to a steep concrete ramp. It is badly broken up, exposed, and usually covered with pebbles, but cartop and inflatable boats can be launched here in calm weather. The road continues until mile 13, arriving at La Bufadora, which has a number of restaurants and arts and crafts businesses. There is a steep, very rough ramp at La Bufadora, suitable only for cartoppers and inflatables.

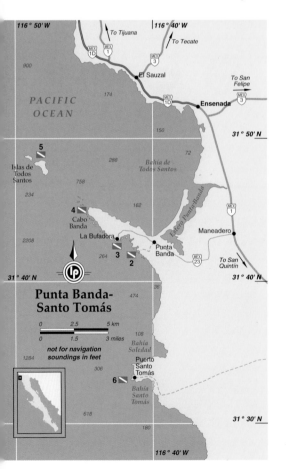

WALT PETERSON

A diver's kayak is useful at sites with good beach access, such as La Bufadora.

Their safety and low freeboard make inflatables popular with Baja divers and snorkelers.

WALT PETERSON

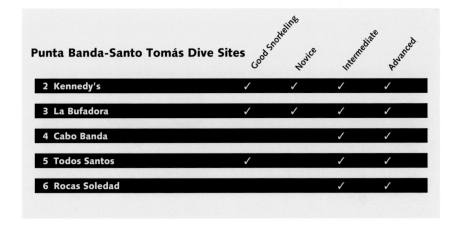

Punta Banda-Santo Tomás Dive Sites	Good Snorkeling	Novice	Intermediate	Advanced
2 Kennedy's	✓	✓	✓	✓
3 La Bufadora	✓	✓	✓	✓
4 Cabo Banda			✓	✓
5 Todos Santos	✓		✓	✓
6 Rocas Soledad			✓	✓

2 Kennedy's

Kennedy's is one of the most beautiful diving areas in Baja California [Norte]. Located on the southwest side of the Punta Banda peninsula, it offers fine underwater and topside photography. The calm and sheltered waters make Kennedy's an ideal spot for novice divers and snorkelers.

Strikingly beautiful green anemones are found at Kennedy's. Shaped like a mushroom, the species is actually an animal related to the corals and gorgonians. Its single opening serves as

Expertise Rating: Novice
Access: Beach dive
Depth Range: Shallow-60 ft (18 meters)
Temperature: W/S: 57/62°F (14/17°C)
Visibility: W/S: 30/20 ft (9/6 meters)

both mouth and anus and it attaches itself to rocks with a muscular foot. The anemone gets its green color from the algae in its tissues, which provides oxygen and energy via photosynthesis. In return, the algae receive nutrients, carbon dioxide, and protection from the anemone. Out of light, in caves and shaded locations, the anemones are nearly pure white. Seemingly inert, they are quick enough to catch small fish and crabs to supplement their diet of plankton. With large discs that can expand to 10 inches, the anemones are exceeded in size only by an Australian species.

To get to Kennedy's, drive to mile 8 on the Punta Banda road, turn left (south) on the dirt road signed COLONEL ESTEBAN CANTU and reset odometer. Turn right at mile 0.5, and at mile 1 make a left at the concrete-block shed. The road down the southwestern spine of the peninsula has loose rock and fairly steep slopes. Once at the cove, you will have to climb down rocky slopes to get to the cobble beach. Small boats and inflatables can be lowered on ropes. Along the coast there are a number of sea caves, arches and blowholes. The bottom is well picked over by commercial divers, but you'll still be able to find much marine life, especially inedible species that have been left alone by commercial hunters.

3 La Bufadora

Due to prolific marine life, an easy beach entry and only two hours' driving time from Southern California, La Bufadora is one of the most popular dive sites along Baja's Pacific coast. The bottom is mixed boulders, cobble and sand, covered with dense kelp beds.

Photographers should watch for the dozen species of nudibranchs that have been identified here. Nudibranchs are gastropods and are closely related to snails. Small and delicate-looking, they are actually rather well-armed. Some species secrete digestive juices that dissolve prey before it is swallowed, and many excrete acids or foul-tasting mucus to repel attackers. They are often brightly colored, which serves as a warning to predators and almost all are hermaphrodites, having both male and female reproductive organs. Some have digestive systems that do strange things: They are able to swallow prey that is armed with nematocysts (tiny capsules containing a stinger) but rather

Expertise Rating: Novice

Access: Beach dive

Depth Range: Shallow-90 ft (27 meters)

Temperature W/S: 57/62°F (14/17°C)

Visibility W/S: 30/20 ft (9/6 meters)

than digesting the nematocysts, they are passed internally to the tips of the frills on their backs, where they are used for defense. Some even put nematocysts into their egg masses, an unhappy surprise for any animal attempting to eat them.

Underwater hot springs venting hot water and gas can be found at 70 to 90 ft. You may also be treated to a special encounter with a Pacific seahorse, near the northern limit of its range here. Diving along the coast toward Cabo Banda is excellent, as marine life becomes denser with each mile.

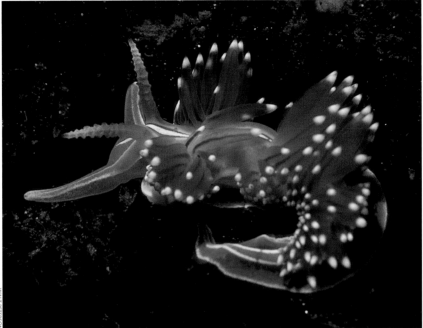

The stunning *Hermissenda* nudibranch can be found in the
Northern Pacific region and throughout the Cortez.

The Pacific seahorse ranges from San Diego to Peru, including the Cortez.
Most are very small, but a few grow up to 12 inches long.

El Niño, the "Boy Child"

El Niño is a condition that results when sea surface temperatures are above normal off the west coast of South America. Causing drastic disruptions of local fisheries, the warm water drives fish into deeper waters or away from their usual habitat. In addition, it alters the general circulation of the Pacific Ocean and the atmosphere, affecting the frequency and severity of storms. Some scientists believe it is responsible for floods and hurricanes in Africa, Argentina, China, India, Japan and the U.S. El Niño was blamed when recent drought and forest fires devastated Indonesia and Brazil. It has even been named as one of the causes of the French Revolution (1789-99), when farmers demanding aid during an El Niño-induced drought were refused by the government.

El Niño has recently affected fish along the west coast of North America. In 1993, several Cortez angelfish, a more tropical species, were seen in the San Diego area. In 1997 fishing boats caught dolphinfish off San Francisco and a marlin was caught off Washington state.

Kelp forests take a beating during El Niño years, but have a history of bouncing back.

In Baja, during non-El Niño years, Isla San Benito West has a dense kelp "jungle" off its southern shore, but during the winter of 1997, El Niño reduced it to more of a desert than a jungle. The 1997-98 winter whale-watching season in the Bahía Magdalena was poorly attended by the whales, while the lagoons farther north were crowded with them. El Niño was again blamed for the odd behavior; the whales just kept swimming south until the water was warm enough for their reproductive rites and then they simply stopped.

4 Cabo Banda

The dive site off Cabo Banda is a series of pinnacles stretching for over a mile toward Islas de Todos Santos. The end of the pinnacles is marked by a navigational light. With sheer rock walls, cliffs and ledges, Cabo Banda is the top site in the Ensenada area. Currents sweep past, carrying astronomical numbers of plankton and other small creatures, which attract dozens—perhaps hundreds—of other species.

One fish that seems to defy Darwin's law of "survival of the fittest" is the garibaldi. Growing up to a foot long, adults are bright orange in color, an attribute that would seem to attract predators. But, like other brightly colored animals, their color may actually be a warning to predators that they taste bad or are dangerous. Unlike many fish species, male garibaldis prepare the nesting site and then guard it after the female lays the eggs.

Although near the southern end of their

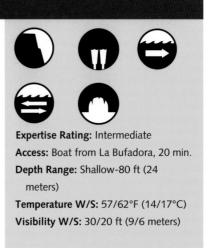

Expertise Rating: Intermediate
Access: Boat from La Bufadora, 20 min.
Depth Range: Shallow-80 ft (24 meters)
Temperature W/S: 57/62°F (14/17°C)
Visibility W/S: 30/20 ft (9/6 meters)

range at Isla San Martin, California red anemones are still prolific. They do not like sunshine and cluster under ledges and inside caves. Many caves and crevices also harbor California spiny lobsters, which will shoot out like roman candles when they feel trapped.

WALT PETERSON

The brightly colored garibaldi is a common Cabo Banda inhabitant.

WALT PETERSON

Red anemones dislike sunlight so it's best to photograph them at night, when they open.

5 Todos Santos

Islas de Todos Santos consist of two islands, the northwest one flat and featureless, the southeast one rugged and much higher. An abalone farm occupies a cove on the east side of the southeast island. The islands are far enough offshore that the visibility is usually good.

Expertise Rating: Intermediate
Access: Boat from Ensenada, 1 hr; boat from La Bufadora, 45 min.
Depth Range: Shallow-80 ft (24 meters)
Temperature W/S: 57/62°F (14/17°C)
Visibility W/S: 40/30 ft, (12/9 meters)

Divers and snorkelers mostly visit the eastern sides of the islands due to their calm and protected conditions, but the turbulent western sides have the most prolific underwater life.

One of the most common species is the yellowtail. Watch for fish with blue-gray to olive backs and silver-white bellies, with a yellow stripe from head to tail. Yellowtail can get very big in Baja waters, up to almost 80 pounds. They like to hang around rocky points, headlands and reefs, rather than flat, featureless underwater terrain and are often found under kelp paddies. They feed in the morning and late afternoon on small fish, crabs and squid. Yellowtail are very unpredictable when confronted by a diver or snorkeler; if crazed by the sight of squid or small fish, they seem to ignore everything else and you can approach quite close. At other times, they will spook at the sight of you. Should this occur, their curiosity sometimes lures them back long enough for a photograph. Wiggle your fingers or tap on a scuba tank with a knife to get their attention. The species is found along Baja's Pacific coast and in the Cortez; large ones generally hang around all year, but the smaller ones form schools, migrate north in the warm months and head south in the fall.

There is excellent diving and snorkeling all around both islands, although the waves on the western side of the northwest island are often too large—the area is known to surfers as *El Martillo* (The Hammer), for good reason. Because of its shallow depths and the profusion of life, the channel between the two islands offers fine snorkeling and diving during calm weather in 10 to 30 ft. Snorkeling is excellent around the south end of the south island.

LOUISA PRESTON

Yellowtails are swift fish that rarely hang around long enough for a photo.

6 Rocas Soledad

Sheer walls, tiny caves, crevices, pinnacles, abundant wildlife and excellent visibility make Rocas Soledad the best dive site between Punta Banda and Roca Ben. With several species of scallops and abalone hiding in deep crevices and colorful schools of fish, all set off by the deep blue of surrounding depths, this site provides a field day for photographers. A wide-angle lens will be useful here. The snorkeling potential is very low, although free-divers could enjoy this site. Expect a light-to-moderate current to the south and beware, the surge can be heavy.

To get to Rocas Soledad, drive to KM 47+ on the Transpeninsular Highway south of Ensenada, turn west onto the graded dirt road, and set odometer. The road reaches La Bocana at mile 17.1, swings north after climbing a short, steep stretch of concrete road, arriving at Puerto Santo

Expertise Rating: Intermediate

Access: Boat from Santo Tomás, 10 min

Depth Range: Shallow-130 ft (40 meters)

Temperature W/S: 57/62°F (14/17°C)

Visibility W/S: 60/40 ft (18/12 meters)

WALT PETERSON

Mexican panga divers prepare to gather sea urchins.

Tomás at mile 19.8. Pangas (open fiber-glass skiffs) can be rented and boats can be launched at a steep concrete launch ramp during high tides and calm conditions. Parking and camping are usually not a problem. Rocas Soledad is 1.25 miles west of Punta Santo Tomás. A shelf extending 40-150 yards south of Rocas Soledad makes it possible to anchor in 40-70 ft.

A tiny red abalone struts its stuff.

Baja's Commercial Divers

Baja California is home to a relatively large number of professional divers, most employed by the abalone, sea cucumber and sea urchin fisheries along the Pacific coast. The divers operate from pangas, which are about 20 feet long and powered by 40 h.p. outboards. The boats are equipped with a shallow-water dive rig consisting of a cast-off refrigeration compressor driven by a small gasoline engine, a volume tank made from a stainless steel beer keg, several hundred feet of hose and a battered scuba second stage. Few, if any, are rated for diving by their manufacturers, and no filters or oil separators are used.

There are fewer professional divers in the Cortez, since abalone and edible sea urchins are absent. About ten years ago large numbers of *almehas voladores* ("flying clams" that are actually a species of scallop) were found near Bahía de los Ángeles. The beds were quickly wiped out. A similar pillage has wreaked havoc on the clams and scallops of Bahía Concepción, with similar results. At least one operation has been busy illegally taking small fish from Cortez waters for the pleasure of aquarium fanciers in the U.S.

Mexican urchin divers load the day's catch at Puerto Santo Tomás. The urchins' sex organs will be removed and flown to Japan, where they are a prized delicacy.

San Quintín Area

Two offshore seamounts south of Isla San Martín—Johnston's Seamount and Roca Ben—are the best scuba sites between Rocas Soledad and Sacramento Reef. The San Quintín area marks the southern limit of a number of cool-water species, such as the lingcod, and the northern extent of warm water fish, such as the blunthead triggerfish.

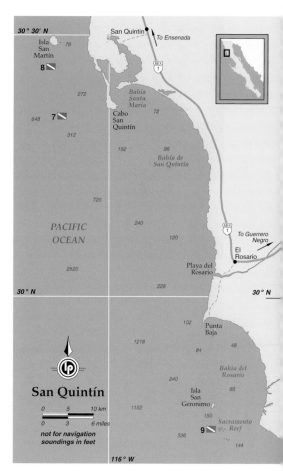

To get to the San Quintín area, drive to San Quintín, 186 miles (299 km) south of the Tijuana border crossing on the Transpeninsular Highway. Turn west on the graded sedan road opposite a large electrical station. Set odometer and arrive at the Old Mill at mile 3.4. There is a motel, RV park, restaurant and boat ramp here, and you can rent pangas and cruisers. Watch the weather and the tides carefully and use care to stay in the channel of the inside bay. With the exception of the *Horizon* from San Diego, no dive operations currently visit the San Quintín area.

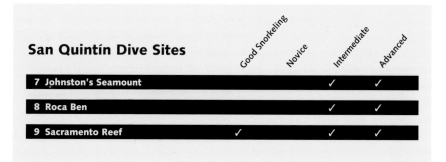

San Quintín Dive Sites

	Good Snorkeling	Novice	Intermediate	Advanced
7 Johnston's Seamount			✓	✓
8 Roca Ben			✓	✓
9 Sacramento Reef	✓		✓	✓

A photographer focuses on a tiny creature in the kelp forest
at Hassler's Cove, Isla San Martín.

7 Johnston's Seamount

Johnston's Seamount is 6 miles, 240° from Cabo San Quintín, the southern tip of the peninsula that forms the western margin of Bahía San Quintín. You'll know you're over the site when Mount Mazo, the low peak just north of the cape, bears 52° and the peak on San Martín bears 340°. The seamount has two pinnacles, one of which rises to within 10 ft of the surface, the other to within 55 ft.

The most unusual feature here—and at Roca Ben to the north—is the profusion of large mussels that thrive on the southern sides down to 80 ft. Divers may encounter numerous species of fish—especially in the summer—and lucky ones may glimpse a billfish or yellowfin tuna. Graced with many fish species and normally excellent visibility, Johnston's Seamount is a renowned location for wide-angle underwater photography. Because of the problems in anchoring here, it may be best to set up a drift dive.

Expertise Rating: Intermediate

Access: Boat from the Old Mill near San Quintín, 1½ hrs

Depth Range: 10-130 ft (3-40 meters)

Temperature W/S: 58/63°F (14/17°C)

Visibility W/S: 80/50 ft (24/15 meters)

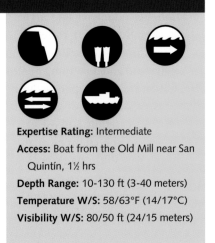

Painted greenlings often hover motionless, unseen by divers and predators.

The kelp rockfish is found in Northern Pacific kelp forests, where its habit of resting head-up or head-down has earned it the name "Dumb Bass."

8 Roca Ben

Roca Ben, 2½ miles south of San Martín, is a rocky pinnacle rising to within 12 ft of the surface at low tide. The scenery is magnificent, the deep blue of surrounding depths contrasts with the green sea grass, colorful sea stars, sea urchins and hydrocorals studding the sheer walls. The site is frequented by the same species of fish as Johnston's Seamount, as well as exceptionally large corrugated and green abalone.

Surf boils sometimes mark its location, but a compass fix may be helpful; when over the site, Mount Mazo will bear 110° and the peak on San Martín 346°. Take

Expertise Rating: Intermediate

Access: Boat from the Old Mill near San Quintín, 1½ hrs

Depth Range: 12-130 ft (4-40 meters)

Temperature W/S: 58/63°F (14/17°C)

Visibility W/S: 80/50 ft (24/15 meters)

WALT PETERSON

Sea cucumbers are considered a delicacy in Japan and Southeast Asia.

great care while diving here. In 1987, the charter fishing vessel *Fish 'N Fool* was rolled over by a huge breaker near Roca Ben and 10 people were killed. The vessel now rests in 165 ft, too deep for sport divers to view. Do not approach the site unless it is flat calm, and stand off at least a half-hour to determine if there are any "sneaker" waves coming in. Free-divers could access a few interesting areas, but there is little potential for snorkeling. A light-to-moderate current to the south can be expected and surge can be heavy. It may be best to set up a drift dive.

9 Sacramento Reef

Three miles southeast of Isla San Geronimo, Sacramento Reef has been described as a "seething cauldron of Hell," a name earned by the many vessels that have wrecked here, including the big U.S. side-wheel steamer *Sacramento*. Wrecked in December 1872, the *Sacramento* carried a treasure of gold and silver coins and bullion. The passengers made it safely to Geronimo and were put aboard another vessel. The gold? Newspapers of the day claimed the treasure was completely recovered, but sea urchin divers may show you photos of small bars, which they claim to be gold taken from the wreck of the "muy rico yate" (very rich yacht) *Goodwill*, lost in 1969. However, the location they describe is actually that of the *Sacramento*.

The *Sacramento* lies scattered just south of the easternmost in a series of islets forming the southern margin of the reef. If you can't find it, ask one of the locals to take you to Roca Timón (Rudder Rock). It is covered with heavy plant and coral growth. Huge timbers lie partly buried in sand and divers have found onyx door-knobs, china, silverware, coins, brass

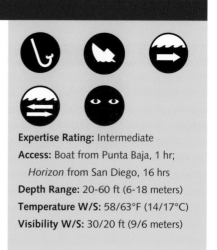

Expertise Rating: Intermediate
Access: Boat from Punta Baja, 1 hr; *Horizon* from San Diego, 16 hrs
Depth Range: 20-60 ft (6-18 meters)
Temperature W/S: 58/63°F (14/17°C)
Visibility W/S: 30/20 ft (9/6 meters)

valves, large vases, sailor's buttons and bottles near the wreck. Many other wrecks rest nearby and divers often have a hard time figuring out which wreck is which.

Despite its bad name among sailors, a more appropriate description of the reef would be a "seething cauldron of life." Dense surf grass—with blades up to 12 ft long—is home to great numbers of horn sharks. Gray sponges reach huge proportions and growths of bryozoans are exceptionally thick. Big giant sea bass, weighing over 550 pounds and reaching 100 years old may be encountered. California spiny lobsters are common, especially on the eastern margins of the reef. Diveable areas of the reef cover several square miles. It is not safe to dive or snorkel if swells exceed 2 or 3 ft, even if you can launch safely off the beach at Punta Baja.

To get to the reef, drive to El Rosario at KM 56 on the Transpeninsular, 226 miles south of the border crossing at Tijuana. At the 90° turn in the highway, turn southwest, take the left fork just before mile .1 and cross the river at mile 0.9. (The right fork leads to a fish-packing plant, which has a recompression chamber.) This crossing is flat and sandy and is usually no problem to drive through. Take the right fork at mile 1, and at mile 2.5 continue straight ahead at the fork. Turn left at the fork at mile 2.9—there's a PUNTA BAJA sign—and arrive at the settlement at mile 10.3. Cartoppers can launch off the beach and pangas may be available for rent. The locals have cut a dirt ramp with a bulldozer, but it is very steep and rough, and its usefulness for launching trailer boats is questionable. The *Horizon* occasionally visits the reef.

WALT PETERSON

California spiny lobsters are found from San Diego to the Cape, and in the Cortez. Unlike their Atlantic cousins, they do not bear large claws.

The majestic green of a blooming kelp forest at the San Benitos.

Southern Pacific Dive Sites

The Southern Pacific region stretches from the San Benitos to the latitude of La Paz. The California Current sets south at about 0.25 knots in this region. A weak counter-current, the Davidson, occasionally runs north along the shoreline between November and January. The average yearly tidal range is about 5.2 ft (2 meters). A trip to the best dive sites in the region requires a considerable investment in time and money—a foray to scout the location of the submarine *H-1* requires a hefty drive and long boat trip, but if you're up for it, the diving is worth the trip. The region has no dive operations, although Cabo San Lucas and La Paz are not far off in the region's southern reaches.

The transition from temperate to tropical forms of marine life continues. The Benitos are a major crossroads for marine creatures. Basket stars, burrito grunts, orangeside triggerfish, pink cardinalfish, rock croakers, scissortail damselfish, spottail grunts, stone scorpionfish and torpedo rays make their first appearances at the Benitos. The islands also mark the southern limit of the beautiful *Hermissenda* nudibranch, the cabezon and the calico rockfish. The red abalone of more northern waters have dwindled in size and numbers here, while the black abalone becomes more numerous.

Hydrocoral and colonial zoanthid clusters along a reef wall.

San Benito Area

Many of the best dive sites in the Southern Pacific region are off Islas San Benito. Because of their remote location, they remain rarely visited even

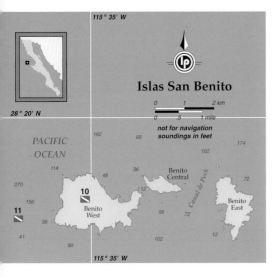

though they are among the best dive sites on Baja's Pacific coast, rivaled only by Sacramento Reef and the seamounts south of San Martín. Visitors usually come here on yachts or as passengers on the *Horizon*, which offers trips to the islands from San Diego. There is a small commercial fishing and diving settlement on the west island. Nearby Isla Cedros and Isla Natividad have settlements and there is a recompression chamber on each island, owned by the local cooperatives.

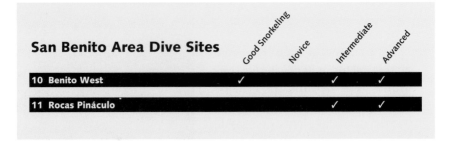

San Benito Area Dive Sites	Good Snorkeling	Novice	Intermediate	Advanced
10 Benito West	✓		✓	✓
11 Rocas Pináculo			✓	✓

10 Benito West

Isla San Benito Oeste (Benito West) has a dense kelp canopy off its southern shore that is home to incredible numbers of fish. A pinnacle southeast of the navigation light on the south side of the island offers the best nature-watching. When you are over the dive site, the light will bear 312° and the south tip of Benito East 76°. A large anchor rests in 50 ft on the sandy bottom, 200 ft off the southeast point of Benito West. When you are over the anchor, the north peak on Benito East will bear 56°, the south end of Benito East 90°, and the cross on top of the hill south of the village on Benito West 293°.

Expertise Rating: Intermediate
Access: Boat from Bahía Tortugas, 4 hrs; *Horizon* from San Diego, 27 hrs
Depth Range: Shallow-70 ft (21 meters)
Temperature W/S: 60/64°F (16/18°C)
Visibility W/S: 60/30 ft (18/9 meters)

Benito West also offers a good wreck dive. In 1934, the 8,200-ton, 464-ft U.S. tanker *Swift Eagle* went aground off the north shore. She lies in shallow water and can be observed by snorkelers. Hull plating is missing in many places, exposing ribs and allowing entry into the hull. You can see anchors, capstans, engine blocks, portholes and lengths of chain. To find her, look for the lighthouse and turn south when it bears 175°.

SUE DIPPOLD

DIANE GEDYMEN

The scissortail damselfish is found in large schools from the Benitos to Peru.

This anchor is an underwater landmark at Isla San Benito Oeste.

11 Rocas Pináculo

Rocas Pináculo (Pinnacle Rocks) are located 1,600 yards west of Benito West. When over the site, the right tangent of the island should bear 91°, the left tangent 40°. Rising almost to the surface from deep water, its two pinnacles are rarely visited and remain unspoiled. Surrounded by deep blue water, the pinacles are excellent for wide-angle photography. The site is completely open; strong currents are common.

This is the best site on Baja's Pacific coast to see white seabass. Watch for a fairly large fish—most average about 20 to 30 lbs, but the largest get up to 83 lbs—with a blue-gray back with dark speckling and a silver belly. They are found along Baja's Pacific coast as far south as Bahía Magdalena and an isolated population lives in the northern Cortez. Despite their large size and relatively high position in the

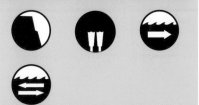

Expertise Rating: Intermediate
Access: Boat from Bahía Tortugas, 4 hrs; *Horizon* from San Diego, 27 hrs
Depth Range: 6-130 ft (2-40 meters)
Temperature W/S: 60/64°F (16/18°C)
Visibility W/S: 60/40 ft (18/12 meters)

food chain, whites spook very easily. Seeming devoid of curiosity, they have a definite aversion to regulator bubbles and will flee at the pop of a strobe. Marlin sometimes appear here in the warm months.

Bahía Magdalena Area

Many ships have wrecked along the shores of the islands forming the western margins of Bahía Magdalena and its southern extension, Bahía Almejas. Trailer boats should launch from the concrete ramp at San Carlos. To get there turn west from Ciudad Constitución at the signed intersection at the north end of town and reach San Carlos at KM 58. The town lacks RV and camping facilities, but flat parking spaces can be found. A recompression chamber has been installed in the Productos Pesquera de Bahía Magdalena plant in town, but its operational status is unclear; so far as it is known, no one is trained to operate it. Drive 0.2 mile northeast from the PEMEX, then southeast for another 1.5 miles, where you'll find the launch ramp. There are several restaurants, food stores and other facilities.

Bahía Magdelena Dive Sites	Good Snorkeling	Novice	Intermediate	Advanced
12 Colombia			✓	✓
13 H-1			✓	✓

The California dorid can be found from Monterey, California to Bahía Magdalena.

WALT PETERSON

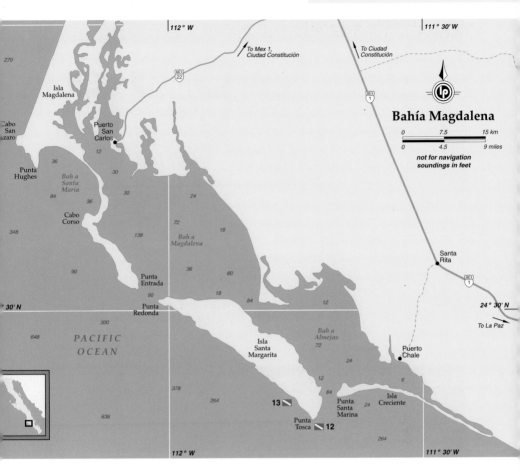

Bahía Magdalena

Divers with portable boats should drive to Santa Rita, KM 157 south of Ciudad Constitución. Turn west on the pickup road and drive 15 miles to Puerto Chale. Sandy protected beaches on the east coast of Isla Santa Margarita provide good camping. No dive operations currently offer trips to the Bahía Magdalena area. Local government officials visit these wreck sites and may require divers to leave.

Bahía Magdalena is another major crossroads for marine life. Blue spiny lobster, Cortez grunt, Cortez round stingray, finespotted jawfish, large-holed sand dollar, leopard grouper, Mexican lookdown, pinto spiny lobster, reef coronetfish, slimy sea slug, and yellow snapper make their first appearances, while the California halibut, California spiny lobster, garibaldi, kelp bass and white seabass, common in the north, dwindle in numbers here.

12 *Colombia*

The 5,643-ton U.S. vessel *Colombia* ran aground at Punta Tosca in 1931, carrying 234 passengers and crew, and $850,000 in gold and silver bars. Everyone was rescued without injury and salvage divers later used dynamite to clear a path to the vaults. However, many believe that substantial amounts of gold and silver remain unrecovered and a number of diving expeditions have been organized over the years to search for the missing treasure. One diver salvaged $2,000 in gold, but a later group, after working for almost two months, recovered nothing. Today, the *Colombia* is badly broken up, with her huge metal plates and ribs lying scattered about.

The ship lies 20 yards east of the last

Expertise Rating: Intermediate at slack water and calm weather

Access: Boat from Puerto Chale, 1 hr; boat from San Carlos, 2 hrs

Depth Range: 50-60 ft (15-18 meters)

Water Temperature W/S: 67/71°F (19/22°C)

Visibility W/S: 50/20 ft (15/6 meters)

wash rock south of Punta Tosca. Large lobsters abound on the wreck. Currents in Canal Rehusa can be very strong, making photography difficult and limited.

The calico rockfish prefers deep water and is at its northernmost limit in the Southern Pacific region.

13 *H-1*

The submarine USS *H-1* was underway in the early morning darkness on March 12, 1920. Thinking that the vessel was near the entrance to the bay, her captain ordered a turn to starboard, and the boat quickly ran aground in the huge breakers. On March 24 the *H-1* was towed off the beach and promptly sank. Due to the hazards and expenses involved in refloating her, she was abandoned and stricken from Navy records. Locating the wreck is one of the great adventures in Baja diving.

She sank in 54 ft at latitude 24° 24' 54" N, longitude 111° 50' 45" W, 9.75 miles northwest of Punta Tosca, on the Pacific side of Isla Santa Margarita. Just after the *H-1* sank, the following was recorded in the log of the USS *Vestal,* one of the salvage vessels: "Rt. peak 100° true. Gorge Rock 315° true." The USS *Brant's* log states "Outer Twin Sisters bearing 119° true, Point Toscok [Tosca] 130° 30' true." Most of these names and locations appear on marine chart 21121, "Rt. peak" apparently being the 1,631 ft peak and "Gorge

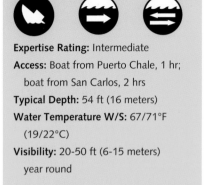

Expertise Rating: Intermediate

Access: Boat from Puerto Chale, 1 hr; boat from San Carlos, 2 hrs

Typical Depth: 54 ft (16 meters)

Water Temperature W/S: 67/71°F (19/22°C)

Visibility: 20-50 ft (6-15 meters) year round

Leopard groupers are common in southern Baja waters.

Rock" one of the rocks at the foot of the white bluff.

This is an intermediate dive and only those with special wreck diving training should attempt to enter the wreck.

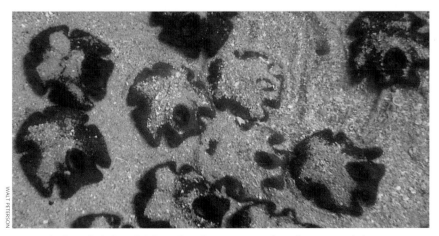

The large-holed sand dollar is found in astronomical numbers on sandy bottoms throughout the Cortez, and from Bahía Magdalena to the Cape.

Northern Cortez Dive Sites

The Northern Cortez region extends from the north end of the Cortez to Isla San Pedro Mártir, including the Midriff area. The tides are a major concern in this region. Beginning at roughly the latitude of Santa Rosalía, tidal ranges increase rapidly, the average annual tidal range being 7.7 ft (2.3 meters) at Bahía San Francisquito and 8.1 ft (2.5 meters) at Bahía de los Ángeles. At the mouth of the Río Colorado, near San Felipe, the tidal range reaches an astonishing 31 ft (9.5 meters). The tidal range can make boat launching problematic. Since low tides uncover vast mud flats, the water's edge may be almost out of sight from the launch ramp. These extremes, plus the billions of tons of silt that have been carried into the Cortez by the Colorado over the millenniums, can greatly reduce visibility in the northern end of the Cortez. Farther south, tidal currents can reach six knots as they squeeze past the islands in the Midriff area, causing whirlpools so powerful that a boat can be spun in a full circle in seconds. The Northern Cortez region is currently home to only two dive operations, the **Bahía San Francisquito Resort** and **Charters Mar de Cortez**.

San Felipe

By means of a huge tidal range and limited visibility, Mother Nature has insured that San Felipe is of limited interest to most divers. However, Charters Mar de Cortez can provide compressed air, rental equipment, and instruction. As the town is lively, interesting and close to the border, San Felipe attracts divers, many of whom are beginners or novices. The best dive sites are at the Islas Encantadas, about 63 miles south of town.

All diving and snorkeling trips in San Felipe must be planned with the tide tables. There are usable concrete launch ramps at the **El Cortez Motel** and the **Club de Pesca**, and **Ruben's Trailer Park** has special vehicles for across-the-beach launches. The town has numerous RV parks, hotels and restaurants. To drive to San Felipe, cross the border at Tijuana or Tecate, and take Route 2 or 2D east to the Route 3 intersection, or cross the border at Mexicali and drive to the same intersection. From this point, drive south on Route 3 to San Felipe.

Bahía de los Ángeles Area

Bahía de los Ángeles offers the first really good diving south of San Felipe; the tidal range is much less, the visibility better and the underwater life far more diverse and prolific.

To get to Bahía de los Ángeles, drive to Parador Punta Prieta at KM 280 on the Transpeninsular. Turn east from the Transpeninsular onto the paved road and arrive at the town at 40 miles from Punta Prieta. **Costa del Sol** has the nicest accommodations in town and the **Villa Vitta Motel**, just to the south, has a bar, a pool and a restaurant. There are a number of campgrounds in the vicinity, including **Villa Vitta RV Park, Guillermo's RV Park, Daggett's Campground** and **Gecko Campground**. Restaurants include **Casa Diaz, Restaurant las Hamacas** and one at Guillermo's RV Park. There is no dive shop or reliable source of compressed air.

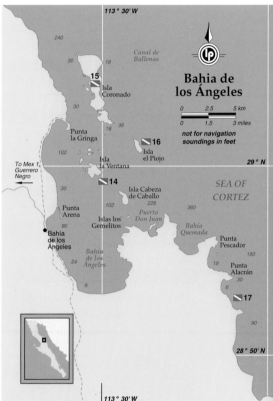

Bahía de los Ángeles Dive Sites	Good Snorkeling	Novice	Intermediate	Advanced
14 *Marcelo*	✓	✓	✓	✓
15 **Isla Coronado**	✓	✓	✓	✓
16 **Piojo**	✓	✓	✓	✓
17 **Racito**	✓	✓	✓	✓

Bahía de los Ángeles is a rather strange place from the standpoint of its marine life. An uncommonly large number of species inhabit the bay and it is not unusual to see 30 or more species in a day of diving or snorkeling. Among the fish present are barberfish, barspot cardinalfish, blue-and-yellow chromis, browncheek blenny, Cortez angelfish, Cortez damselfish, Cortez garden eel, Cortez halibut, finescale triggerfish, glasseye, Gulf grouper, lizard triplefin, ocean whitefish, Panamic soldierfish, sheephead, sierra, spotted cabrilla, spotted sand bass, threebanded butterflyfish, white seabass, yellowfin croaker, yellowtail and various rays and rockfish. The bay's invertebrates include the California spiny lobster, flower urchin, *Hermissenda* nudibranch, sea pen, slate pencil urchin, Spanish shawl nudibranch, tidepool shrimp and tan sea star.

Some of these species don't seem to belong here, such as ocean whitefish, California spiny lobster, sheephead and white seabass, which are "Southern California" critters. There is a simple answer: Although early explorers thought Baja to be an island, there has been no direct connection between the Northern Cortez region and the Pacific at any point in the geological history of the peninsula. Some Baja residents claim there is a tunnel under the peninsula that connects the Cortez and the Pacific, but a more likely reason is that the ancestors of these species began during a period when Cortez waters were cooler. Some species in the bay are distinctly tropical, like barberfish, threebanded butterflyfish and flower urchin. These are examples of the strange mix of the tropical and the temperate in the Cortez.

Male browncheek blennies signal their availability for romance by jerking their heads in and out of their little burrows.

Sate pencil urchins often wedge their thick, blunt spines into crevices, making it difficult for predators to extract them.

14 *Marcelo*

The reef between Isla Ventana and Isla Cabeza de Caballo got its name from the 50-ft fishing vessel *Marcelo*, wrecked there in 1983. Lying 400 yards southeast of the "window" landmark on Ventana, the reef is about 100 yards long. Deeper sections have the most colorful sea life in the bay. Watch for warm-water barberfish and cold-water ocean whitefish, further examples of the odd assembly of creatures in the bay. The reef is bordered by flat sandy areas, where you can spot halibut, rays and Panamic pen shells. These bivalves get very large—up to 2 ft long and 5 inches across—and are usually found buried in sand with their long axis vertical and only the upper rims of their shells visible. They contain a large amount of flesh that would be edible

Expertise Rating: Novice

Access: Boat from Bahía de los Ángeles, 20 min.

Depth Range: 10-50 ft (3-15 meters)

Water Temperature W/S: 59/79°F (15/26°C)

Visibility W/S: 60/30 ft (18/9 meters)

except for one fact—it tastes terrible. A half-dozen shallow rock pinnacles are barely covered at moderate tides, so take care when approaching Most of the *Marcelo* is about 20 ft from the southeastern pinnacle.

The graceful sea pen is found on sandy and muddy bottoms.

A diver explores the remnants of a Cortez wreck.

15 Isla Coronado

Isla Coronado, 2.2 miles northeast of Punta la Gringa, has a number of good snorkeling and diving sites, especially on the east side. The bottom is largely boulders and cobble, forming numerous tiny caves and crevices that harbor many fish and invertebrates, including small numbers of brilliantly colored Panamic soldierfish, at the very northern limit of their range. An excellent reef continues from the southeastern tip of the island. There you'll find flower urchins, whose specialized appendages (*pedicellariae*) make them look like gardens of white roses with red centers. Some urchins attempt to disguise themselves by carrying bits of algae and broken shells, but beware, their short spines are venomous.

The west side of Coronado is not as interesting as the east, although the channel between Coronado and Isla Mitlan offers good snorkeling. Coronadito, a tiny islet off the north end of the island, has fine snorkeling on its north and west sides.

Expertise Rating: Novice

Access: Boat from Bahía de los Ángeles, 30 min.

Depth Range: 10-90 ft (3-27 meters)

Water Temperature W/S: 59/79° (15/26°C)

Visibility W/S: 50/25 ft (15/8 meters)

The rock slipper lobster looks like a WWI tank, or perhaps an underwater cockroach.

The strange and beautiful flower urchin is found from the Bahía de los Ángeles area all the way to Ecuador.

16 Piojo

Isla el Piojo (Louse Island) is known for the number and variety of its nudibranchs, making it popular with macro photographers. A 1:1 or 1:2 extension ring and framer will be most useful. The water around the island is not too deep and the bottom is sand. At the end of the dive, if you're out of air but still have some unused film, some free-diving might be in order. Nudibranchs are often found in shallow water, the most common being the brilliant purple and gold Spanish shawl, sometimes found in intertidal zones. Another close relative occasionally encountered includes the clown nudibranch. With a white body covered with red and yellow spots, the species is well-armed against predators. It is also armed with nematocysts, which it obtains by eat-

Expertise Rating: Novice

Access: Boat from Bahía de los Ángeles, 30 min.

Depth Range: Shallow-40 ft (12 meters)

Water Temperature W/S:
59/79°(15/26°C)

Visibility W/S: 50/25 ft (15/8 meters)

ing hydroids and other prey. The clown nudibranch also deters predators with a noxious chemical that it produces after eating sponges. The island is well out in the Cortez and thus receives less shelter from wind, wave and tidal currents, so use care.

WALT PETERSON

This Spanish shawl nudibranch was encountered at Isla Piojo.

17 Racito

In 1981, a fishing vessel burned and sank off the east side of Isla el Racito, a low, rocky islet 700 yards north of Punta el Soldado. While it varies from season to season, the wreck offers one of the best displays of marine life in the Bahía de los Ángeles area, rivaled only by the *Marcelo*. The wreck lies in 10 to 16 ft, about 100 ft off the east side of the island, midway between the north and south points.

Expertise Rating: Novice
Access: Boat from Bahía de los Ángeles, 1½ hrs.
Depth Range: Shallow
Water Temperature W/S: 59/79°F (15/26° C)
Visibility W/S: 50/25 ft (15/8 meters)

Among the most common inhabitants are barberfish, blue-and-yellow chromis, Panamic soldierfish, flower urchins, *Hermissenda* nudibranchs, sea pens and several species of gorgonian and sea fans. Cortez garden eels and Cortez halibut are common in nearby sandy areas. Because it is in very shallow water and in an exposed area, the wreck is disintegrating rapidly and may not last much longer.

The Biggest Fish in the Sea

Human encounters with whale sharks have occurred ever since vessels capable of plying ocean waters were built, but the species was not scientifically described until 1828. Their habit of basking at the surface made them increasingly vulnerable to collisions with ships, which were becoming larger and faster. Whale sharks inevitably lost—one giant was even cut completely in half by a steamer. The heaviest specimen ever recorded was caught in a fish trap in Siam in 1919. It weighed about 90,000 lbs and measured 59-ft-long. They have cartilaginous skeletons, skin four inches thick and dorsal fins that can grow to 6 ft.

TAMMY PELUSO

TAMMY PELUSO

A diver explores a ravine lined with colorful sea fans.

Midriff Area

The Midriff is the informal name given to the islands in the Cortez that extend from the latitude of the north end of Guardian Angel Island south to the latitude of Isla San Pedro Mártir. It includes about 55 islands, islets and pinnacles. The largest, Tiburón, geographically in the state of Sonora, has an area of 385 sq miles. Remote and unspoiled, the Midriff area is uninhabited, except for small camps of commercial divers and fishers, guano collectors and a few game wardens. The Cortez is only about 60 miles (97 km) wide at this point. Tidal currents race by the islands forming giant whirlpools that pull up nutrients from deep waters, which support vast quantities of plankton, which in turn support an extensive food chain. The Midriff is alive with birds and marine mammals; whales include blue, Bryde's, finback, gray, killer, Minke, pygmy sperm and sperm whales. You might also encounter common dolphins and Pacific bottlenose dolphins.

Diving and snorkeling in the Midriff are very different than in areas to the south. Because of the upwellings, water temperatures can be much cooler than those in the southern end of the Cortez. Many species familiar in the Southern Cortez are absent or much reduced in the Midriff, especially some of the small, brightly colored creatures that fall within the term "reef fish." Interesting fish in the Midriff include; finescale triggerfish, giant sea bass, Gulf grouper, Mexican barracuda, skipjack, spotted cabrilla, white seabass, various sharks and marlin. Check out the large population of yellowtail, so plentiful they are often referred to in terms of acreage rather than numbers.

The Midriff is difficult to get to and no dive operators currently offer trips. The nearest places to launch boats are Bahía de los Ángeles, Bahía San Francisquito and Bahía Kino, which is in the state of Sonora. The closest source for compressed air is San Francisquito Resort, so visitors should either

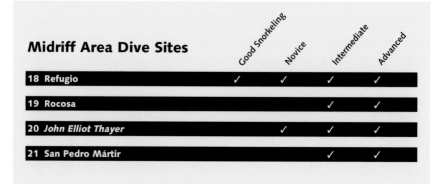

Midriff Area Dive Sites	Good Snorkeling	Novice	Intermediate	Advanced
18 Refugio	✓	✓	✓	✓
19 Rocosa			✓	✓
20 *John Elliot Thayer*		✓	✓	✓
21 San Pedro Mártir			✓	✓

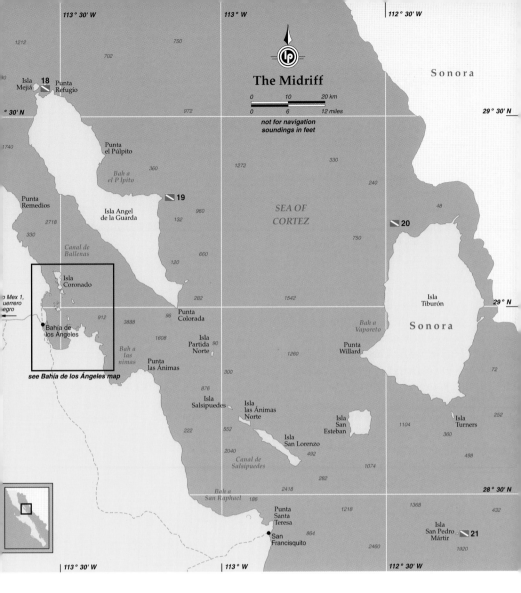

The Midriff

113° 30' W   113° W   112° 30' W

1212   750   702

Isla Mejiá **18** Punta Refugio

Sonora

0   10   20 km
0   6   12 miles

**not for navigation
soundings in feet**

29° 30' N

972

1740

Punta el Púlpito

1272   330

Bahía el Púlpito

360   240

Punta Remedios

19

Isla Angel de la Guarda   132   960

SEA OF CORTEZ

48

20

2718   330

Canal de Ballenas

660   750

120

Isla Coronado

Isla Tiburón

29° N

to Mex 1, Guerrero Negro

912   96   Punta Colorada

282   1542

Bahía Vaporeto   Sonora

Bahía de los Angeles

3888   1608   Isla Partida Norte   90

Punta Willard

72

Bahía las Ánimas   Punta las Ánimas

1260

300

see Bahía de los Ángeles map

876

Isla Salsipuedes   222   552   Isla las Ánimas Norte

Isla San Esteban   1104   Isla Turners   252

360

Isla San Lorenzo   492

2040   *Canal de Salsipuedes*   1074   498

282

2418

Bahía San Raphael   186

28° 30' N

Punta Santa Teresa   1218   1368   432

San Francisquito   864   Isla San Pedro Mártir   **21**

2460   1820

113° 30' W   113° W   112° 30' W

bring a compressor or hooka, or be prepared to enjoy a lot of free-diving and snorkeling. Amenities are extremely limited, including any dependable source of emergency assistance. Be prepared to wait-out the heavy winds in winter. In 1996, a group was stranded on Isla San Lorenzo for more than a week.

To get to San Francisquito, turn northeast at KM 189+, 17 miles southeast of Guerrero Negro. Set odometer. The road is in poor condition, but in 1998 road crews widened and graded the road to a point 10 miles northeast of El Arco. Once you hit mile 25.1, the road passes El Arco, where you can buy fuel, water and food. At mile 61.1 arrive at Rancho el Progreso, marked by a windmill. Turn left and at mile 61.6 and you'll see the resort. You can launch your boat over the sand beach at the inner harbor north of the resort.

18 Refugio

At the north end of Guardian Angel, Bahía Refugio is one of the most scenic parts of the island, underwater and above. It is not often visited by divers, despite the roughly 4 sq miles of bottom within the 130-ft sport diving limit. A three-tank-per-day trip could go on for weeks without ever visiting the same site twice. Snorkelers have over 17 miles of shallow water around the bay's islands and southern shoreline.

There are a few particularly good sites. A reef projecting 800 yards north of Isla Mejía's north point, has numerous wash rocks and boulders that drop down to sand at 70 ft. The eastern and western points of Isla el Granito have much smaller reefs, dropping down to 75 ft. Visibility is normally good during periods of calm winds and when the tidal range is small. Tidal currents can be heavy, especially

Expertise Rating: Novice
Access: Boat from Bahía de los Ángeles, 3 hrs
Depth Range: Shallow-130 ft (40 meters)
Water Temperature W/S: 59/79°F (15/26°C)
Visibility W/S: 40/20 ft (12/6 meters)

near the shallow reefs at the north and south ends of the small island between Mejía and Guardian Angel.

The marine life in Refugio is similar to that described for Bahía de los Ángeles, except for the larger, more abundant lobsters that have escaped the best efforts of local fishermen.

A diver packs up for the next leg of a circumnavigation of Guardian Angel.

19 Rocosa

Punta Rocosa, on the east side of Guardian Angel, about half way between the north and south ends of the island, is a very specialized dive site. The heavy tidal currents of the northern Cortez, the roughly northwest/southeast orientation of the island's mountains, the "hook" shape of the coastline to the west and north, and the prevailing north winds often combine to turn Rocosa into a churning melee of wind, water and waves. Whirlpools can spin boats—and divers—around in circles. The energy and direction of the whirlpools often cause "piles" of water that can reach over a foot high. The underwater regions off the point are not particularly beautiful, generally lacking colorful sea stars, gorgonians and bright reef fish. Why would anyone of sound mind wish to dive such a place? The answer is simple: big fish. Fishy predators, often including huge Gulf groupers, move

Expertise Rating: Intermediate
Access: Boat from Bahía de los Ángeles, 3 hrs.
Depth Range: Shallow-80 ft (24 meters)
Water Temperature W/S: 59°/79°F (15/26°C)
Visibility W/S: 50/30 ft (15/9 meters)

in to feed and sometimes hang around in slack water, making Rocosa one of the premier sites in the Cortez for encountering big fish.

Rocosa is not safe to dive in anything but slack water and then only by Intermediate and Advanced divers. Setting up a drift dive is unwise; it is better to wait for slack water or to choose a safer site.

WALT PETERSON

An almost solid wall of bigeye jacks swimming in the Cortez.

20 *John Elliott Thayer*

Expertise Rating: Novice

Access: Boat from Bahía de los Ángeles, 4 hrs; boat from Bahía Kino, Sonora, 3½ hrs

Depth Range: 45-55 ft (14/17 meters)

Water Temperature W/S: 60/79°F (16/26°C)

Visibility W/S: 40/30 ft (12/9 meters)

In 1858, the full-rigged U.S. sailing ship *John Elliott Thayer* burned at anchor while loading guano at Isla Patos. She was the victim of arson by a disgruntled crew member. Today, the *Thayer* is one of the best wreck dives in the Cortez, with easily visible huge wooden timbers and thick planking. Strewn about the wreck you can see glass bottles, silverware, three types of ceramic plates, bronze spikes and copper sheathing, a huge iron capstan, anchors, an iron object that was perhaps a gaff-jaw, a large metallic ring, brass sailor buttons and iron harpoons. Lima Mint Charles III 8-escudo coins dated 1780 have been recovered from the wreck. She can sometimes be seen from the surface, but the snorkeling potential is very low. Except for the wreck, the site is not terribly photogenic.

No dive operations offer trips to the wreck. To get to Patos, launch your boat at Bahía de los Ángeles or Bahía Kino, Sonora, the distances being about 68 and 49 miles, respectively. The *Thayer* is 320° from the aids-to-navigation light on Patos, 283° from a rocky outcrop forming its southwest cape and 53° from the left tangent of a small island south of Punta Sargento.

THE PEABODY ESSEX MUSEUM

John Elliot Thayer packet ship arriving off Prince's Dock, Liverpool, 1857.

Did Someone Say Shark?

WALT STEARNS

Although their numbers are dwindling due to over-fishing, sharks are still plentiful in Baja, especially in the Southern Cortez region. A number of years ago, 425 sharks were caught in 27 hours in one net at El Barril. Great whites occur in the Cortez, much to the uneasiness of divers. Although shark incidents are very rare in Baja waters, they do happen. When the paddle-wheel steamer *Continental* sank off Cabo San Lucas in 1870, a man stood on something solid for a moment when his raft turned over, only to have it shoot away—it was a large shark, apparently looking for lunch. While diving on the *Shasta,* a small wreck just south of Isla Creciente, a diver was suddenly surrounded by a swarm of aggressive sharks and had to climb the wreck's mast, which was fortunately still sticking out of the water. During a dive on the *John Elliott Thayer* in 1983, divers towing a disabled boat were buzzed by a large shark, resulting in a mad scramble back into the boat.

21 San Pedro Mártir

Isla San Pedro Mártir attracts fewer divers than any island in the Cortez. About 1 sq-mile in area and 1,000 ft high, it is located 22 miles south of Isla Tiburón. Since the island is surrounded by deep water and subject to heavy currents, tidal mixing causes plankton to thrive, supporting an extensive food chain. Since rainfall averages only three inches a year, guano collects year after year, giving the island an iceberg appearance from a distance. In the 1880s, 135 Yaqui Indians and their families lived on the island, mining guano for an American company—an unusual setting for a human settlement.

Expertise Rating: Intermediate

Access: Boat from Bahía de los Ángeles, 5 hrs; boat from Bahía San Francis-quito, 2 hrs; boat from Kino, Sonora, 2½ hrs

Depth Range: 20-60 ft (6-18 meters)

Water Temperature W/S: 60/76°F (16/24°C) occasionally colder upwellings

Visibility W/S: 60/40 ft (18/12 meters)

Diving areas are limited, since depths in excess of 200 ft are encountered within a dozen yards around much of the island. However, two islets at the south end have a sizable area with good diving at 20 to 60 ft. The bottom is jumbled cobble, boulders and shelf rock. Another small dive site is found along the western side, where the bottom drops steeply with a series of ledges and small caves. Large fish sometime appear, including the Gulf grouper. Warm-water Moorish idols are sometimes reported, despite the occasional deep upwellings that bring up very cold water. The areas suitable for snorkeling are quite small.

Packing up after a week-long trip to Isla Turners, just south of Isla Tiburón. Fortunately, on this trip, the Cortez was almost flat-calm.

Southern Cortez Dive Sites

The Southern Cortez region extends from the latitude of Isla San Pedro Mártir to that of La Paz. The annual tidal range averages only about 3.2 ft (1 meter), and tidal currents are thus less swift than in the Northern Cortez, making the diving safer and the visibility better. Marine life here is distinctly different from that to the north. The Southern Cortez region can be much deeper—plummeting to 14,000 ft (4,267 meters) in one location—with much more stable water temperatures. As in many parts of the world, the marine biomass (the total weight of all living matter) tends to be higher in northern waters than in the southern, even though the number of species is higher in southern waters. In the Southern Cortez, Cape and Revillagigedos regions, this increase in diversity becomes more apparent and "new" species appear more frequently. The more interesting fish include azure parrotfish, bluechin parrotfish, Cortez rainbow wrasse, dorado, dusky sergeant major, flag cabrilla, gafftopsail pompano, giant damselfish, giant hawkfish, glasseye, guineafowl puffer,

With gold and blue bands on their sides, juvenile king angelfish at first appear to be a separate species. A curious moray watches with interest.

TAMMY PELUSO

The guineafowl puffer's appearance was perhaps designed to make predators die of laughter.

jewel moray, jewfish, king angelfish, longnose butterflyfish, Moorish idol, Pacific manta ray, Panamic green moray and zebra moray. Many of the species found in the Southern Cortez have strong tropical affinities; a few range as far south as Ecuador. Spotted sand bass, so abundant in the Northern Cortez, are not likely to appear here, nor are the "California" fish seen at Bahía de los Ángeles.

The invertebrates are well represented and you are likely to see at least a sampling of the following: arrow crab, pink murex, bluestriped sea slug, Bradley's sea star, California sea hare, elegant coral, elegant hermit crab, flower urchin, giant coral, Lucas' cleaner shrimp, orange cup coral, Panamic crown-of-thorns, Panamic pearl oyster, purplelip rock oyster, sea pen, slate pencil urchin, slipper lobster and yellow polyp black coral.

Because the dive sites tend to cluster, the Southern Cortez region is broken down into four areas: Santa Rosalía, Mulegé, Loreto and La Paz. Mulegé is pronounced Mool-ah-**hay**.

Night Dive

A night dive in the Southern Cortez region will introduce you to a number of marine animals that you may never have seen before and perhaps don't even know exist: sand anemones, formless blobs during the day, become beauties at night. Panamic soldierfish and tinsel squirrelfish, reclusive in the backs of caves and crevices during the day are brilliant flashes of red and silver after dark; jewel morays, with their distinctive patterns of gold and brown, glitter like jewels; Panamic green morays, whose bodies can reach six feet long, and two or three species of shrimp and lobster, unseen during the day, magically appear at dusk.

WALT PETERSON

The Panamic soldierfish (red) and the tinsel squirrelfish (silver) both like dark caves and are often found hanging out together.

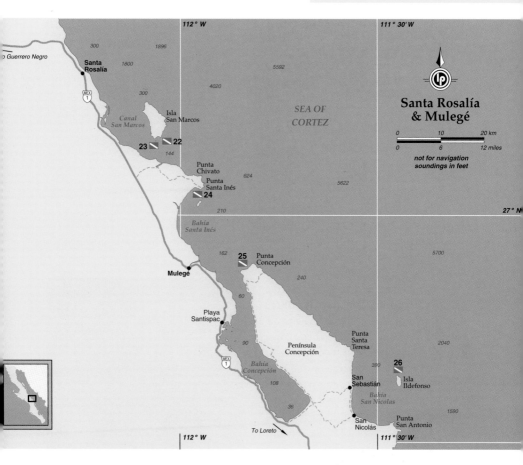

Santa Rosalía Area

A number of restaurants, hotels, motels, food stores and other facilities are available in Santa Rosalía, but there are currently no dive operations or paved launch ramps. The best dive sites are Isla San Marcos and Lobos.

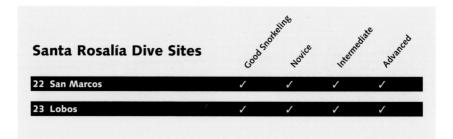

Santa Rosalía Dive Sites	Good Snorkeling	Novice	Intermediate	Advanced
22 San Marcos	✓	✓	✓	✓
23 Lobos	✓	✓	✓	✓

22 San Marcos

Isla San Marcos is the site of a major gypsum mine. Large ships load at the pier on the western side of the island and carry the material to countries around the Pacific, where it is made into drywall and other products. The best diving site is at the north end, where a shallow reef of jumbled boulders extends for 800 yards, some of which above the water.

The industrial nature of the island does not seem to have harmed the marine life and divers may easily encounter several dozen species on a single dive. The handsome giant hawkfish appears occasionally in the more shallow areas of the reef and lucky visitors may spot three species of morays, including the Panamic green, the jewel and the zebra. For a month or two each year, two species of damselfish seem to emerge on the reef; one is under 2 inches-long, iridescent blue with a black spot just below the dorsal fin, the other is a drab brown and about 4 or 5 inches-long. Despite very different appearances, both are Cortez damselfish. Immature fish are blue, turning to brown as they age. Trailer boats can be launched at Chivato and portable boats at the San Lucas Trailer Park at KM 182 on the Transpeninsular.

Expertise Rating: Novice

Access: Boat from San Lucas Trailer Park, 30 min.; from Chivato, 45 min.

Depth Range: Shallow-60 ft (18 meters)

Water Temperature W/S: 59/79°F (15/26°C)

Visibility W/S: 60/30 ft (18/9 meters)

The color and pattern of a zebra moray are unmistakable.

Panamic green morays can look hazardous, but most only wish to be left alone.

23 Lobos

The reef that extends south from Isla San Marcos about 1,500 yards to Roca Lobos is one of the best snorkeling and shallow-water diving areas in the Southern Cortez region. The chaotic jumble of boulders, cobbles, crevices, ledges and patches of sand provide many micro-environments and observant divers and snorkelers may see 30 or 40 species in a day. If you see what seems to be a spider, with long, spindly legs and a pink or reddish body about a half-inch across, it is probably an arrow crab. Should you encounter a red-colored sea star with short, rounded spines it may be a Bradley's sea star. This species has the disconcerting habit of casting off one or more of its arms when stressed. The arm continues to wiggle for a while to distract predators from the rest of the animal.

Expertise Rating: Novice

Access: Boat from San Lucas Trailer Park, 30 min.; boat from Chivato, 45 min.

Depth Range: Shallow-70 ft (21 meters)

Water Temperature W/S: 59/79°F (15/26°C)

Visibility W/S: 60/30 ft (18/9 meters)

Trailer boats can be launched in Mulegé and portable boats at the San Lucas Trailer Park at KM 182. Time spent running boats can be reduced to a minimum by camping on Lobos.

A Bradley's sea star and a synapted cucumber. The sea star will readily cast off one or more arms if disturbed.

Mulegé Area

There are hotels, RV parks, restaurants and other amenities in Mulegé, located at KM 135+ on the Transpeninsular Highway. The original Mulegé Divers has broken into two separate businesses, **Cortez Explorers** and **The Shop**. Cortez Explorers provides dive trips, rentals and a resort course. The Shop sells a selection of diving equipment, as well as books, T-shirts and fishing equipment. Launch ramps are available at several of the RV parks on the south side of the "river" in Mulegé and at the **Hotel Serenidad**.

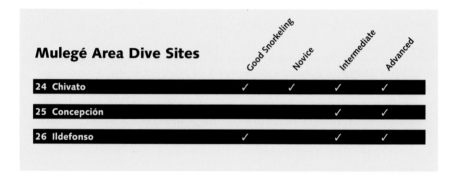

Mulegé Area Dive Sites	Good Snorkeling	Novice	Intermediate	Advanced
24 Chivato	✓	✓	✓	✓
25 Concepción			✓	✓
26 Ildefonso	✓		✓	✓

24 Chivato

To get to Chivato, turn northeast on the sandy road off the Transpeninsular at KM 156, 13 miles north of Mulegé. Follow the sandy road for 14 miles. The campground to the east of the hotel is in a beautiful location, but offers no electrical or water hookups. There are plans to build homes and the campsite could be moved to a lesser site. The Hotel Punta Chivato has a restaurant, bar and pool. There is a tiny grocery store nearby and a concrete launch ramp west of the hotel. Heavy winds are frequent from December through February.

A shallow reef that extends a hundred yards from shore clockwise from Punta Chivato past Punta Santa Inéz is a favorite with snorkelers. There is an unidentified wreck between the two points. The Islas Santa Inés—a group of tiny islands two

Expertise Rating: Novice
Access: Beach; Boat to Islas Santa Inés from Chivato, 10 min.; boat from Mulegé, 45 min.
Depth Range: Shallow-70 ft (21 meters)
Water Temperature W/S: 59/79°F (15/26°C)
Visibility W/S: 50/30 ft (15/9 meters)

miles southeast of the point—offers some of the best diving and snorkeling in the Mulegé area. The Mexican fishing vessel *Britania*, lost in 1980, lies 150 ft east and 300-400 ft south of the northern tip of the south island in 5 to 15 ft. The historic schooner *Abel Miranda*, built in 1859 and sunk in 1957, is believed to lie somewhere in the vicinity. Cortez Explorers offers boat trips to the islands.

Judging by the immense numbers of shells cast up on the beach to the west of the hotel, the bay in front of the hotel must be covered with mollusks. The pink murex, among the most common, has a shell in the traditional "seashell" shape. It grows up to 6 inches-long and the inside of the opening is pink or red. There are at least 30 species of shrimp in Cortez waters. Few are seen during the day, but at night they come out to forage. On a night dive at Chivato you likely see three or four species, the most likely being the tidepool shrimp. This small creature has an almost transparent shell, through which you can see its inner workings. Its body is marked by a series of black, longitudinal stripes and its legs have red bands.

25 Concepción

Cortez Explorers makes frequent boat trips to the excellent diving and snorkeling sites near Punta Concepción. Although Mulegé looks like the stereotypical tropical village, with its palms and thatched roofs, the Tropic of Cancer lies far to the south.

Still, the underwater life continues to change and you'll encounter increasing numbers of "tropical" creatures, such as the Cortez rainbow wrasse, jewel moray and gafftopsail pompano. Also watch for the orange cup coral, a tropical species found from this area south to Ecuador. Ranging up to a foot in diameter and between orange and yellow in color, the colonies are usually found in shady locations from just below the surface to about 60 ft. At first glance, the species does not seem to be a coral at all, lacking the hard exterior "skeletons" of the yellow polyp black, elegant and giant corals found in the Cortez to the south, but a coral it is, consisting of separate animals fused together at their bases. Concepción is completely exposed to north weather and is sometimes un-divable for a week at a time in the winter months.

Expertise Rating: Intermediate
Access: Boat from Mulegé, 45 min.
Depth Range: Shallow-80 ft (24 meters)
Water Temperature W/S: 62/83°
  (17/28°C)
Visibility W/S: 40/30 ft (12/9 meters)

WALT STEARNS

Orange cup coral is common under ledges, boulders and other shaded areas.

26 Ildefonso

The reefs at the north and south ends of Isla Ildefonso are the best dive spots around the island. Both have great pinnacles and walls covered with sessile marine life. Look closely for the purplelip rock oyster. Despite its size—the species is one of the largest bivalves in the Cortez, sometimes reaching 10 inches across—it is very difficult to spot, at least until you learn what to look for. Keep an eye out for what appears to be an ordinary rock sitting on top of a boulder or attached to its side. The oyster's upper shell is often heavily encrusted, but it can be identified by the purple bands inside the margins of its shell. If a large, deeply ribbed bivalve is found on rubble or in sand, it is probably a Pacific lion's paw, the largest scallop in the Cortez. Both species are taken in large numbers by commercial divers, but because of the isolation of the island, they are still found here, for now.

Because it is located 45 miles from Mulegé by boat, the island sees few divers. There is a ranch on the east shore of Península Concepción that can be reached

Expertise Rating: Intermediate

Access: Boat from Mulegé, 3 hrs; boat from San Sebastián, 30 min.

Depth Range: 40-60 ft (12-18 meters)

Water Temperature W/S: 62/83°F (17/28°C)

Visibility W/S: 40/30 ft (12/9 meters)

by pickup. To get to San Sebastián drive past KM 76+ on the Transpeninsular, 36 miles south of Mulegé, turn east on the dirt road and set odometer. At mile 5.5 take the left fork and at mile 5.6 take the right fork and arrive at San Sebastián at mile 14.6. San Sebastián consists of just a few ranch buildings, a number parked trailers and shaded campsites, although you might be able to hire a panga. Ildefonso is 8 miles east of the cove and small boats can be launched over the steep pebble beach. Snorkeling in the cove is excellent.

WALT PETERSON

The purplelip rock oyster is among the largest of the Cortez bivalves.

Loreto Area

Although legislation establishing the "National Marine Park, Bay of Loreto" was passed, so far no money has been allocated for enforcement, and its status remains uncertain. Its rough boundaries include Islas Coronados at the north end and Isla Santa Catalina to the south, extending 25 miles (40 km) east of the Baja coastline. Trailer boats can be launched at the public ramp at the small, man-made harbor in Loreto, or at Puerto Escondido, 16 miles (26 km) to the south. Portable boats can also be launched over the sand beach at the north end of town and just south of **Loreto Shores Villas & RV Park**. Local dive operations currently include **Aqua Sports de Loreto**, **Deportes Blazer**, **Arturo's Sports Fishing Fleet** and **Baja Outpost**. Loreto has an international airport and there are numerous hotels, RV parks, restaurants and other facilities.

TAMMY PELUSO

The small harbor at Loreto.

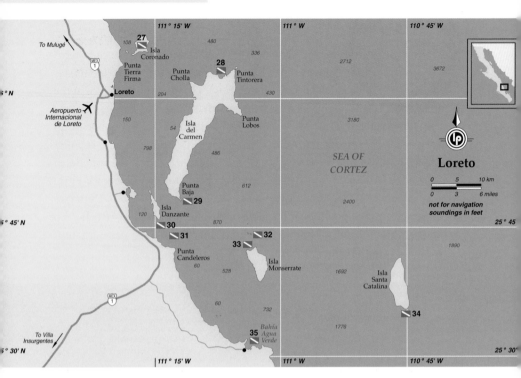

Loreto Area Dive Sites	Good Snorkeling	Novice	Intermediate	Advanced
27 Islas Coronados	✓	✓	✓	✓
28 Carmen North		✓	✓	✓
29 Carmen South	✓	✓	✓	✓
30 Danzante	✓	✓	✓	✓
31 Los Candeleros			✓	✓
32 La Reinita			✓	✓
33 Monserrate	✓		✓	✓
34 Catalina	✓		✓	✓
35 Agua Verde	✓		✓	✓

27 Islas Coronados

Islas Coronados consist of a small volcanic island and a tiny islet just to the west. Five miles north of Loreto, the island's southeast side has a sand beach and calm water that attract many picnickers, brought from Loreto by panga. The sandy bottom off this beach, with patches of rocks and boulders, is also a popular snorkeling site, and there are rocky reefs extending from the island's northeast and southeast ends.

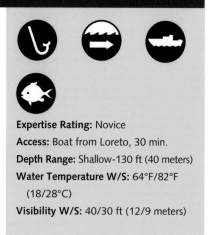

Expertise Rating: Novice

Access: Boat from Loreto, 30 min.

Depth Range: Shallow-130 ft (40 meters)

Water Temperature W/S: 64°F/82°F (18/28°C)

Visibility W/S: 40/30 ft (12/9 meters)

One of the most common fish here and in many other parts of the Cortez is the sergeant major, which can grow up to 9 inches-long. Sporting five or six vertical black bars, a yellow back and a silvery belly, they are members of the damselfish family, which also includes the scissortail and Cortez damselfish, also found in the Cortez. They are territorial and pugnacious, driving off predators that approach their eggs, sometimes even challenging divers. They often form mixed schools with other species, especially the Cortez chub. If you see a dark-metallic-blue fish that otherwise appears to be a sergeant major, it is a male ready to pursue romance.

The best diving is off the north end of the island, where the bottom is a jumble of boulders, sloping down from 30 ft to deep waters. Currents can be heavy here, so either dive at slack water, set up a drift dive, or stick near the south shore.

WALT PETERSON

If you haven't seen numerous sergeant majors all day, you haven't been looking too hard. The males turn metallic blue when romance seems imminent.

28 Carmen North

Carmen North extends west from Punta Lobos to Isla Cholla at the northwest end of Isla Carmen. The underwater terrain is a chaotic jumble of boulders, ledges and sandy areas. Like most Cortez islands, the marine life at the north end of the island is generally less colorful but larger than in the south.

Expertise Rating: Novice, except for the caves
Access: Boat from Loreto, 1 hr
Depth Range: Shallow-90 ft (27 meters)
Water Temperature W/S: 64/82°F (18/28°C)
Visibility W/S: 40/25 ft (12/8 meters)

The pink cardinalfish and the elegant hermit crab make their first appearances here. Divers from higher latitudes often think that all hermit crabs are small, drab creatures, scuttling around in tiny shells. But here elegant hermit crabs will prove them wrong; with bright pink and red bands and carapaces that can reach 3 inches, some elegant hermits require shells as large as *Murex* or *Strombus*. They prefer rather shallow water—a few even choose the intertidal area—so snorkelers have a good chance of encountering them. This species is one of the most common hermits in the Cortez, ranging from this area south to Ecuador. It is second in size only to the less colorful giant hermit crab, which also inhabits *Murex* and *Strombus* shells and has a similar range.

There are at least nine sea caves near Punta Lobos and west as far Isla Cholla, where the coast of the island turns south. One of them has a 30-ft underwater tunnel. Two caves have extensive air chambers, which expel large volumes of air during periods of heavy surge. In calm weather, qualified divers and experienced free-divers can have great fun exploring these caves.

Elegant hermit crabs hide their elegance in cast-off shells.

29 Carmen South

A relatively shallow reef extending south from Punta Baja, the south tip of Isla Carmen, offers fine diving and snorkeling. Toward the southern end of the reef, a pinnacle comes to within 12 ft of the surface and the water is often crowded with fry and mysids (tiny shrimp-like creatures). The island is the first place where heads of elegant coral and giant coral—prolific at Pulmo Reef—begin to appear. Cortez conches, one of the largest gastropods in the sea, are occasionally encountered in sandy areas off the island (at least those that have eluded the stew pot—the species is popular with the locals).

Expertise Rating: Novice

Access: Boat from Loreto, 1 hr; boat from Escondido, 30 min.

Depth Range: Shallow-70 ft (21 meters)

Water Temperature W/S: 64/82°F (18/28°C)

Visibility W/S: 40/25 ft (12/8 meters)

If you encounter an animal that can only be described as a formless blob and that shoots "ink" at you, it is not necessarily an octopus—it might be a California sea hare. They range in size from 6 inches to over 2 ft in length and are found throughout the Cortez and along Baja's Pacific coast, usually on fairly shallow sandy bottoms. They use their purple ink to deter predators. Large anemones have swallowed sea hares whole, but all is not lost, for once inside, the sea hare releases its ink, causing the anemone to cough up its dinner. Both species seem to escape the ordeal unharmed.

WALT PETERSON

California sea hares emit a dense cloud of purple "ink" when threatened. They are hemaphroditic, each individual having both male and female organs. Romance can last for several days.

30 Danzante

Divers and snorkelers on independent trips who plan to camp on Isla Danzante may find its sand beaches to be occupied by kayakers and *pepino* (sea cucumber) divers. Diving is best on the reef on the island's south cape, where garden eels appear in the sand at 65 ft and black coral grows in deeper water.

A number of fish and invertebrates are near the northern edge of their ranges, including the beaubrummel, bluechin parrotfish, bumphead parrotfish and the slimy sea slug. During the warm months dorado, one of nature's most elegant and mysterious fish, appear in the area. Found throughout the world in tropical and warm temperate seas, they are migratory and tend to travel in schools. Extremely beautiful, they have iridescent blue backs, compressed flanks and a dorsal fin running from over the eyes to the tail fin. The males have high,

Expertise Rating: Novice
Access: Boat from Escondido, 20 min.
Depth Range: Shallow-130 ft (40 meters)
Water Temperature W/S: 64°F/82°F (18/28°C)
Visibility W/S: 40/25 ft (12/8 meters)

almost bump-like, foreheads. Freshly caught dorado often turn the color and sheen of gold lamé, with waves of blue and green shimmering over their entire bodies. They are sold commercially as mahi-mahi. Their reaction to divers and snorkelers ranges from indifference to stark terror, but occasionally schools will approach closely, a rare and special experience.

The bluechin parrotfish is found from Isla Carmen to Ecuador.

WALT PETERSON

31 Los Candeleros

Los Candeleros (The Candlesticks) are a group of rocky islets about 1.5 miles southeast of Danzante. They are not often visited by divers, in spite of their proximity to beaches with good road access. They tend to be most frequented by sports fishers attracted by the large number of fish and the nearness to Escondido.

The site is deep and divers will find steep drop-offs, ending in large boulders. The fine underwater topography, plus the normally excellent visibility, make this a good site for wide-angle photography. Because of the steep sides, snorkeling is very limited, although there is a relatively shallow spot near the middle pinnacle. The marine animals are much the same as at nearby Danzante. None of the local dive shops regularly schedule

Expertise Rating: Intermediate
Access: Boat from beach near Ligui, 10 min.; boat from Escondido, 30 min.
Depth Range: 30-130 ft (9-40 meters)
Water Temperature W/S: 64/82°F (18/28°C)
Visibility W/S: 60/40 ft (18/12 meters)

trips to Candeleros. Divers traveling by private vehicles should turn east at Rancho Ligui, just past KM 84+, south of Loreto. This road passes a number of beaches where portable boats can be launched, and ends at Ensenada Blanca.

32 La Reinita

La Reinita, a small group of islets two miles north of Isla Monserrate, offers the best diving in the Loreto area and all of the local dive operations make trips here. There numerous rocky ledges, shelf rock and jumbled boulders, but the pinnacle walls drop quickly beyond safe depths. The water between the two islets is fairly shallow and great for snorkelers.

Marine life is very similar to Danzante and Candeleros, except for the beautiful blue-and-gold snapper, at the northern limit of its range, often encountered swimming in large schools. You might also notice a fish with unlikely dimensions cruising just under the surface. Often 2 or 3 ft long and just a few inches in height, needlefish use their silver color and odd proportions to make themselves almost invisible to their prey. Their bod-

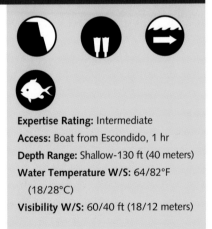

Expertise Rating: Intermediate
Access: Boat from Escondido, 1 hr
Depth Range: Shallow-130 ft (40 meters)
Water Temperature W/S: 64/82°F (18/28°C)
Visibility W/S: 60/40 ft (18/12 meters)

ies enable them to camouflage against the patterns of waves, ripples and sunshine at the surface. A number of related species are found in Baja waters along both coasts.

33 Monserrate

Isla Monserrate attracts few divers, despite being close to the excellent boat ramp at Escondido. The island looks largely barren, but surrounding waters teem with fish and lobsters. The best diving is on the reefs between the two north capes of the island and the reef running southeast from its south end. The bottom at the north end consists of rocky shelves and boulders, dropping slowly to 75 ft and a sandy bottom. The large, shallow reef of alternating fingers of rock and sand is the best place around the island for snorkelers, and all of the site is a prime location for a night dive.

Watch for the bicolor parrotfish, whose range begins here and extends south to Ecuador. Also look for Panamic pearl oysters. This species produced the pearls that early adventurers sought and

Expertise Rating: Intermediate

Access: Boat from Escondido, 1 hr

Depth Range: Shallow-75 ft (23 meters)

Water Temperature W/S: 64/82°F (18/28°C)

Visibility W/S: 60/40 ft (18/12 meters)

which established a large industry in La Paz in the 1800s. The species soon became scarce and virtually all were wiped out by a blight in 1940. They seem

WALT PETERSON

Schools of gregarious blue-and-gold snappers are encountered at Isla Monserrate.

TAMMY PELUSO

A diver admires the sea fans off Loreto.

to be making a comeback, however, and are now found in fair numbers in some locations. Look for a thin, scaly gray shell, usually 4 to 8 inches across and attached to rocks by byssal fibers, with the rims of both shells deeply fluted.

Survival of the Fittest

During a night dive, several divers on a foray out of Loreto saw an unusual sight: a moray attacking an octopus. For over ten minutes the enthralled divers saw nothing but a rolling, boiling ball of green and red, but the moray finally won.

34 Catalina

Isla Santa Catalina marks the approximate southern boundary of the National Marine Park. Lying 14 miles to the east of Monserrate, it sees even fewer divers and snorkelers, although Baja Outpost in Loreto offers trips here. The best diving and snorkeling is off the south cape, where large boulders and ledges produce dramatic underwater scenery. The bottoms off the east side of the island are precipitous, less than those to the west.

Catalina is probably the first place as you head south where you have a chance at seeing an exotic Moorish idol. With an ornate color scheme of black, yellow and white, a protruding snout and a long filament trailing the top of the dorsal fin, this species can not be mistaken for any other. Usually found in pairs, it is occasionally seen in small schools in the Cape region and schools of more than two dozen have been spotted at the Revillagigedos. The species is found in many other locations around the globe.

The island is a regular stop for cruise vessels on natural history trips. Passengers learn about the famous rattle-less rattle snakes and a species of barrel cactus that can reach 10 ft in height and 3 ft in diameter.

Expertise Rating: Intermediate

Access: Boat from Escondido, 2 hrs

Depth Range: Shallow-90 ft (27 meters)

Water Temperature W/S: 64/82°F (18/28°C)

Visibility W/S: 60/40 ft (18/12 meters)

Catalina's Mystery Ships

Over the years, Catalina has been the focus of interest by at least three groups of adventurous scuba divers. Local legend has it that a British vessel, possibly two, sank off the east side of the island somewhere "near a sand spit." British ships voyaged to Santa Rosalía during the copper-mining days, but there is no record of any having wrecked near Catalina. No other British vessels had a valid reason for being in the Cortez, which leads treasure-seekers to believe the ship was up to no good and thus must have been carrying something of value.

MICHAEL PETERSON

Moorish idols are found from Isla Catalina to Ecuador and throughout the Indo-Pacific.

35 Agua Verde

Bahía Agua Verde can be reached by driving to KM 63+ on the Transpeninsular, 35 miles south of Loreto. The unpaved road is graded and improved, but there are a number of hairpin turns and steep slopes. It reaches beach level at mile 14.4, continuing southeast along the shore. The beaches are mostly steep cobble, although short stretches of sand can be found near the settlement at Agua Verde. The road closely parallels the water, but side roads leading to the beaches where portable boats can be launched are limited. The village of Agua Verde is at mile 26.1.

In addition to providing access to Monseratte and Catalina, Agua Verde has its own dive sites. One of the largest black-coral "forests" in the Cortez can be found in 80 to 130 ft off the rocky pinnacle of Roca Solitaria, a 115-ft-high pinnacle at the mouth of the bay. Look for what appear to be bushes bearing tiny yellow flowers, anchored to rocks. The specimens are not very large, but in more favorable habitats in very deep water to the south, they can approach tree-like proportions. The "skeleton" of the coral is a lustrous, dense, jet-black material. Despite its protected status, bracelets, pins and earrings made from it are still sold in the tourist towns in the Cape region. It illegal to import the substance into the U.S. and Canada.

Punta Marcial, where the coastline turns sharply to the south, has excellent diving. A tiny island with a navigation light, located about a mile north of the point, marks the outer fringes of a reef. This reef extends to the south of the point as well, providing a large diveable area down to about 60 to 80 ft. Portions of the reef are shallow enough to please snorkelers.

Expertise Rating: Intermediate

Access: Beach; boat from Escondido, 1½ hrs

Depth Range: Shallow-130 ft (40 meters)

Water Temperature W/S: 64/82°F (18/28°C)

Visibility W/S: 60/40 ft (18/12 meters)

A diver checks out a prolific growth of yellow polyp black coral.

La Paz Area

Because the few divers and snorkelers that visit Isla Santa Cruz arrive by boat from La Paz, rather than Loreto, the island marks the northern extent of the La Paz area. There are currently eight dive operations in the area, all in La Paz: **Baja Diving & Service**, **Baja Expeditions**, **Beach Club El Tecolote**, **Centro de Buceo Cary**, **Cortez Club**, **La Paz Diving Service**, **Scu-Baja Diving Center** and **Scuba Baja Joe**.

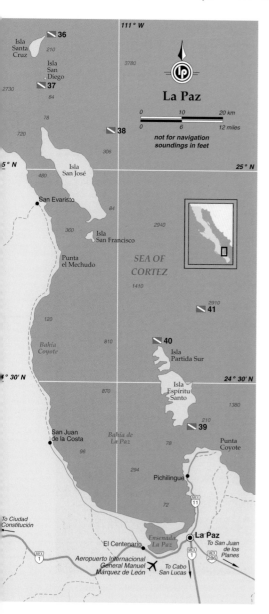

Some of these have high-speed boats that take less time getting to the dive sites to the north than the times shown below. La Paz has a full range of hotels, motels, RV parks, restaurants, supermarkets, as well as an international airport. Boats can be launched at Aquamarina RV Park, Marina de La Paz, Marina Palmira and Marina Pichilingue. In addition there is public launch ramp at KM 18 on the road to Pichilingue.

A kayaker explores the waters around La Paz.

WALT STEARNS

Snorkelers explore Ensenada Balandra, just north of La Paz. The famous balancing rock fell over some time ago, but has since been put back in place.

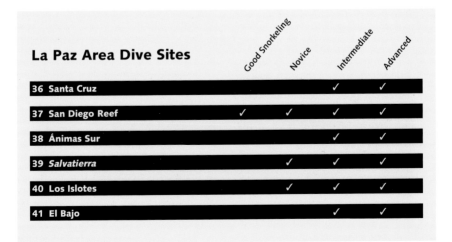

La Paz Area Dive Sites	Good Snorkeling	Novice	Intermediate	Advanced
36 Santa Cruz			✓	✓
37 San Diego Reef	✓	✓	✓	✓
38 Ánimas Sur			✓	✓
39 *Salvatierra*	✓		✓	✓
40 Los Islotes	✓		✓	✓
41 El Bajo			✓	✓

36 Santa Cruz

Being one of the more remote islands in the Cortez, Isla Santa Cruz is not often visited by divers or snorkelers. Its north shore offers the best diving, where the boulders and ledges quickly drop at a steep angle to sand at about 120 ft.

The island marks the northern end of the range for the tiger reef eel in the Cortez, creatures that sometimes cause divers to flee back to the boat believing they are being pursued by sea snakes. The species is named for its tiger-like colors—large black spots separated by areas of yellow—and its lack of a tail fin, which makes it look snake-like. The species is related to the morays and is normally

Expertise Rating: Intermediate
Access: Boat from Escondido, 3 hrs;
  boat from La Paz, 5 hrs
Depth Range: Shallow-120 ft (37 meters)
Water Temperature W/S: 64/82°F
  (18/28°C)
Visibility W/S: 60/40 ft (18/12 meters)

found in shallow waters, where it buries itself in the sand during the day, coming out to hunt at night.

37 San Diego Reef

There are a number of fine diving and snorkeling sites around Isla San Diego, but the southwest reef transcends them all. With intricate lava formations honeycombed by grottos and bright sand bottoms, the marine life on the reef make excellent photographic subjects. An especially fine grotto system can be found in 30 to 40 ft near two pinnacles, awash about 500 yards southwest of the island. For several years a gigantic grouper has made the grotto home and nurse sharks are often seen dozing on the floor. Divers and snorkelers should watch for the comical guineafowl puffer and the sinister Panamic crown-of-thorns, both at the northern limits of their range.

The frogfish is an oddity occasionally seen in the area. Because analogies fail —no other fish looks like it—and no adjectives are up to the task, it is difficult to describe. The species is so formless and ill-defined, with numerous flaps of skin and other

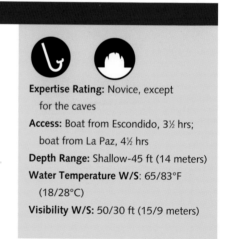

Expertise Rating: Novice, except
  for the caves
Access: Boat from Escondido, 3½ hrs;
  boat from La Paz, 4½ hrs
Depth Range: Shallow-45 ft (14 meters)
Water Temperature W/S: 65/83°F
  (18/28°C)
Visibility W/S: 50/30 ft (15/9 meters)

appendages sprouting from its body, that most divers have never spotted one. Colors don't help, for the critter can be orange, yellow, black, or red, either solid or mottled, in stripes, filaments and fringes. It can change colors in only a few minutes, which allows it to mimic its surroundings. This camouflage allows frogfish to avoid predators and enables them to go "fishing" for their meals. Its "fishing rod" (the modified first dorsal ray) protrudes from the skull, equipped with a "lure" that looks like a worm. When a small fish, seeing nothing dangerous nearby, moves in to take the bait, the frogfish's great mouth opens wide in a fraction of a second, sucking the victim inside, so fast that other fish in the area often do not seem to notice the absence of one of their numbers. When searching for frogfish, don't look for a fish; rather concentrate on looking for just eyes and a large, up-turned mouth. The species in the Cortez is also found on the Pacific coast.

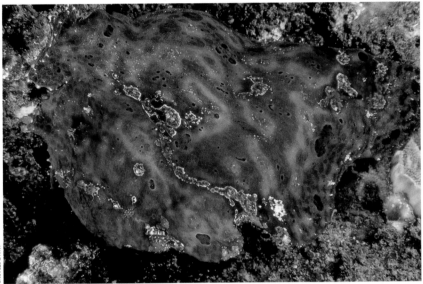

Believe it or not, the reddish object is actually a fish—a frogfish—encountered at San Diego Reef. These odd-looking critters are found in shallow waters world wide.

38 Ánimas Sur

Isla las Ánimas Sur is located 9 miles east of Punta Calabozo, the north point on Isla San José. Surrounded by deep water and very small in area, it is one of the premier deep dives in the Cortez. Its sheer sides plunge almost vertically far past the sport diver's limit of 130 ft. The number and variety of species present, from clouds of tiny fry to colorful reef fish and large pelagics, is exceeded by few other dives in the Cortez.

There are three areas of interest: the island itself; a series of small pinnacles off

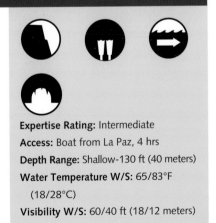

Expertise Rating: Intermediate
Access: Boat from La Paz, 4 hrs
Depth Range: Shallow-130 ft (40 meters)
Water Temperature W/S: 65/83°F
(18/28°C)
Visibility W/S: 60/40 ft (18/12 meters)

its northwest side; and a flat area to the south. So steep is the area that it is difficult to anchor safely, although in calm weather boats can anchor off the south side.

The island has a number of caves, the largest and most interesting found on the northeast side at 80 ft. It goes to near-complete darkness and a light is needed for safety and to see the brilliant colors of the cave occupants. The pinnacles on the northwest side drop down from the surface past a number of ledges and small caves. The bottom to the south of the island starts at about 48 ft, sloping to unsafe depths. Several dive operations in La Paz visit Ánimas Sur.

A diver explores the stern of the *Salvatierra*.

WALT STEARNS

39 *Salvatierra*

In 1976, the *Salvatierra*, an ex-U.S. Navy WWII LST (Landing Ship Transport), sank in Canal de San Lorenzo, about a mile south of Isla Espíritu Santo. It is now one of the best dive sites in the La Paz area.

Large numbers of fish hide under the ship's stern, often so dense you literally have to brush them aside to swim through. If you are really lucky, you might see a longnose butterflyfish or a Clarion angelfish, both found in very limited numbers from here to Cabo San Lucas and in larger numbers at the Revillagigedos.

The ship was used as a ferry between La Paz and Topolobampo on the mainland and was carrying a cargo of trucks and trailers when she sank. Remnants of some of the vehicles can be seen scattered over the sandy bottom. Strong tidal currents are possible in the channel, requiring divers to plan their activities using the tide tables. All dive shops in La Paz organize trips to the wreck.

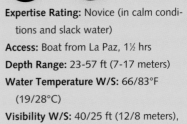

Expertise Rating: Novice (in calm conditions and slack water)

Access: Boat from La Paz, 1½ hrs

Depth Range: 23-57 ft (7-17 meters)

Water Temperature W/S: 66/83°F (19/28°C)

Visibility W/S: 40/25 ft (12/8 meters), occasionally less in heavy currents

WALT PETERSON

The longnose butterflyfish is certainly one of Mother Nature's most exotic creations.

DAVID LEVITT

Shafts of light create a ghostly apparition through a *Salvatierra* porthole.

40 Los Islotes

Los Islotes is one of the "Big Three" of diving in the La Paz area, the other two being the *Salvatierra* and El Bajo. Los Islotes are a group of tiny islets just north of Isla Partida Sur and the great attraction is a colony of friendly sea lions. These animals put on a wonderful show of underwater acrobatics for divers, often doing barrel rolls around them and indulging in a one-sided game of "chicken," where they rush in and veer off at the last second. They will occasionally nip at fins and blow bubbles when almost eye-to-eye with divers. There is limited snorkeling close to shore. A reef abounding with fish and gorgonians starts 800 yards southwest. All dive operators in La Paz organize trips to Los Islotes.

Expertise Rating: Novice

Access: Boat from La Paz, 1½ hrs.

Depth Range: 20-90 ft (6-27 meters)

Water Temperature W/S: 66/83°F (19/28°C)

Visibility W/S: 60/30 ft (18/9 meters)

TAMMY PELUSO

The arch at Los Islotes.

TAMMY PELUSO

California sea lions lounge in a sunbeam.

41 El Bajo

If the amount of television coverage is any gauge, the friendly manta rays and hammerhead sharks have made El Bajo (Marisla Seamount) the most famous dive site in the Cortez. The seamount is located about 8 miles northeast of Los Islotes. Three underwater peaks array along a 300-yard line running northwest/southeast. The northwestern peak rises to within 83 ft of the surface, the central peak to 52 ft and the southeastern to 69 ft. The central peak, with its shallow depths and relatively flat top, is the primary dive site.

Visit El Bajo for reasons other than the mantas, for they are actually very rare and if you have an encounter, consider yourself lucky. The finest months to dive here are August and September. The best time to visit the hammerhead sharks is late summer and early fall, although there is evidence that they may be present year-round. The hammerheads seem to prefer the northwest peak. If the currents turn out to be a problem, set up a drift dive.

Expertise Rating: Intermediate

Access: Boat from La Paz, 2½ hrs

Depth Range: 52-130 ft (16-40 meters)

Water Temperature W/S: 66/83°F (19/28°C)

Visibility W/S: 60/30 ft (18/9 meters)

If you are blowing off excess nitrogen between dives, or if you are a snorkeler, a foray with fins, mask and snorkel to the waters a bit away from the seamount may offer views of some of the large pelagics, including marlin, sailfish dorado and possibly a turtle. All the dive shops in La Paz offer trips to El Bajo, as do the vessels *Don José*, *Río Rita* and *Marisla II*.

TAMMY PELUSO

Dense sea life covers El Bajo.

Getting Together

There seems to be little survival value in schooling for a fish at the top of the food chain. So what advantage do the hammerheads have in congregating? Some scientists think that large, dominant females fight their way to the center of the "school," showing the males that they are the strongest and most desirable mates. Why do they choose El Bajo? The seamount is rich in metals and is known to have a strong magnetic field; hammerheads are believed to be able to sense such fields. So, to answer both questions: the hammerheads congregate as part of a mating ritual and the seamount acts as a beacon.

BILL WARBURTON

Hammerhead sharks look sinister, but they are in fact very shy and will often disappear at the pop of a strobe.

Cape Dive Sites

The Cape region extends from the north end of Isla Cerralvo to the southern tip of the peninsula and around to the southern boundary of the Southern Pacific region. The mean annual tidal range is about 3.1 ft (.9 meters) and tidal currents are correspondingly low. Since the Tropic of Cancer lies just to the north of Cabo Pulmo, all areas to the south are thus "tropical."

The Cape region is one of the world's most prolific fish habitats. A comprehensive list of every species native to the Los Cabos area would fill a substantial book. The most interesting include: banded guitarfish, black skipjack, blue, black and striped marlin, blue-and-yellow chromis, chameleon wrasse, Clarion angelfish, coral hawkfish, dorado, flower urchin, goldrimmed surgeonfish, green jack, jewel moray, longnose hawkfish, Mexican barracuda, Mexican hogfish, Pacific manta, Pacific seahorse, Panamic green moray, Panamic porkfish, sailfish, several species of sea stars, wahoo, yellowfin tuna, zebra moray and various basses. There are also large numbers of sharks, including bull, hammerhead, mako and whale shark. Moorish idols, seen so far along the peninsula alone or in groups of two or three, now form schools twice the size.

East Cape Area

"East Cape" is an informal term applied to the peninsula between Punta Pescadero and somewhere short of San José del Cabo but, for the purposes of this book, it will be expanded to include sites at Isla Cerralvo. There are currently four dive operations in the East Cape area: **Baja Dive Adventures**, **Cabo Pulmo Divers**, **Vista Sea Sports** and **Pepe's Dive Center**. Some of the operations in La Paz also offer trips to the East Cape area. There are numerous resorts, hotels, RV parks, restaurants, food stores and other facilities. **Verdugo's Motel and Trailer Park** and the **Hotel Palmas de Cortez** offer boat launching services. Over-the-beach launches are possible in many places and you'll find a ramp at Pulmo.

Isla Cerralvo is the southernmost island in the Cortez and many of the fish that migrate in and out of the Cortez pass on either side of the island, often very close to shore. The close-packed schools peak in mid-May and again

in October, but large fish like marlin and sailfish sometimes hang around all year.

Ensenada los Muertos provides divers and snorkelers the best boat access to Cerralvo. To get to Muertos, turn east at KM 213 on the Transpeninsular, about 2.5 miles south of the waterfront in La Paz, to Route 286. At KM 43, pass through the village of Los Planes. At KM 48+, take the fork signed ENS DE MUERTOS. Set odometer. The pavement ends at mile 0.2, the road becomes graded and two-lane. At mile 3.7, encounter an intersection; go straight ahead to mile 5.5. There are numerous RV parking sites along the beach, but no facilities. Diving at Muertos is very limited, but a huge anchor, metal rails and ore carts are found scattered over the bottom—mementos of a silver-mining operation in the 1920s.

WALT STEARNS

Encountering a sailfish is a rare treat for divers and snorkelers.

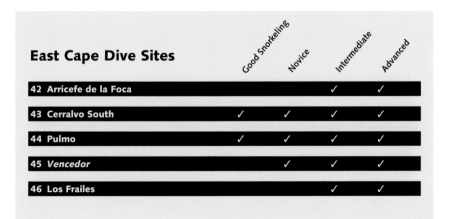

East Cape Dive Sites	Good Snorkeling	Novice	Intermediate	Advanced
42 Arricefe de la Foca			✓	✓
43 Cerralvo South	✓	✓	✓	✓
44 Pulmo	✓	✓	✓	✓
45 *Vencedor*		✓	✓	✓
46 Los Frailes			✓	✓

42 Arricefe de la Foca

About 4 miles north of Isla Cerralvo, a rocky pinnacle sticks out of the water, with a navigational tower on top of it. The surrounding waters are rich in marine life, so much so that California sea lions frequent the place. About 200 yards south of the tower, wreckage from an old ship rests in 70 ft, scattered across a sandy bottom. The word "Mazatlán" can be seen on its stern. The surrounding waters are very deep and it is possible to see large pelagics, such as marlin and sailfish.

A night dive in relatively shallow water is not for the timid; menacing critters are strewn across the bottom, sometimes dozens in just a few square yards. The synapted cucumber has a soft, leathery body of indeterminable length—an adult that seems to be a foot long can stretch out to 4 ft. Unlike more conventional species, it has no fins, feet, or eyes and its "mouth" is fringed with feather-like tentacles used to entangle prey. When touched, the critter will stick to human skin and it may suddenly cleave itself into two or more segments. Other than possibly producing panic attacks, the creatures present little danger to humans. Commercial divers gather other species of cucumber in the Cortez for shipment to Japan where they are considered a delicacy, but there appears to be little demand for this one.

Expertise Rating: Intermediate

Access: Boat from La Paz, 2 hrs; boat from Muertos, 2 hrs

Depth Range: 20-70 ft (6-21 meters)

Water Temperature W/S: 66/83°F (19/28°C)

Visibility W/S: 60/40 ft (18/12 meters)

43 Cerralvo South

The south shore of the island offers excellent diving and snorkeling, especially at Rocas Piedra, marked with sizable boulders as its name implies. A shallow, rocky reef extends out several hundred yards until it ends in sand at about 50 ft. This reef is home to many fish and invertebrates and is sheltered from some of the swift tidal currents that race by both sides of the island. However, for those willing to confine their diving to slack water, the premier site is Roca Montaña, a pinnacle coming to within 6 or 7 ft of the surface, about 1,200 yards south of the southeastern point of the island. The bottom is

Expertise Rating: Novice at slack tide; otherwise Intermediate; advanced south of Roca Montaña

Access: Boat from La Paz, 3 ½ hrs; boat from Muertos, 45 min.; boat from Los Barriles, 2 hrs

Depth Range: Shallow-130 ft (40 meters)

Water Temperature W/S: 66/83°F (19/28°C)

Visibility W/S: 60/40 ft (18/12 meters)

SUE DIPPOLD

This cart is a relic from the silver mining boom
that began in 1862 and ended in 1926.

WALT STEARNS

A diver encounters a "school"
of Panamic sea stars.

crowded with invertebrates, including
Panamic crown-of-thorns, sponges,
hydroids, gorgonians, cowries, conches,
cone shells, nudibranchs, lobsters, crabs,
urchins, sea stars, brittle stars and several
species of coral. Vast beds of garden eels
come to life in sandy areas and black coral
can be found in deep water. The site got its
name when the steamer *Montana* struck
it in 1874, although the ship did not sink.

A bit farther to the south lies one of
Baja's most exciting diving and snorkeling
sites. The attraction is large marlin, sailfish,
wahoo and other big game species. This is
no place for beginners, however, as the
currents can be heavy and erratic. A boat
should always follow such an excursion.
The number of big fish peaks in mid-May
and again in October, but some fish hang
around the entire year.

44 Pulmo

Although there is a tiny reef near Isla Espíritu Santo and many small heads scattered throughout the Southern Cortez region, Pulmo Reef is Baja's only full-fledged coral reef. The residents of the peninsula like to believe it is the only coral reef on the western coast of North America, but the scientific literature describes three others, one in mainland Mexico, one in Costa Rica and one in Panama.

Shielded from the cold Pacific, two species of coral, elegant coral and giant coral, have constructed a sizable reef. Starting near shore just south of Cabo Pulmo and running in a northeasterly direction, broad rows of coral heads continue, ending in about 70 ft. The astronomical

Expertise Rating: Novice

Access: Beach dive; boat to outer sites, 5 min.

Depth Range: Shallow-70 ft (21 meters)

Water Temperature W/S: 68/83°F (20/28°C)

Visibility W/S: 50/60 ft (15/18 meters)

number of nooks, crannies and cavelets formed by the reef are home to an abundance of creatures. In his book *The Log From the Sea of Cortez*, John Steinbeck

A spotted porcupine fish visits the reef at Cabo Pulmo.

TOM HAIGHT

WALT PETERSON

Despite its name, the Cortez angelfish is not a Cortez endemic;
it is also found from Southern California to Peru.

recounted a visit to Pulmo during a 1940 boat trip to collect biological specimens: "The complexity of the life-pattern on Pulmo Reef was even greater than at Cabo San Lucas. Clinging to the coral, growing on it, burrowing into it, was a teeming fauna. Every piece of the soft material broken off skittered and pulsed with life—little crabs and worms and snails. One small piece of coral might conceal 30 or 40 species, and the colors on the reef were electric." Let us hope that Pulmo's status as a National Marine Park saves it from the development that is going on ashore.

Divers will probably see more fish, both in terms of numbers and species, than at many Caribbean sites, especially schooling fish and very large fish. The variety of depths and conditions allows divers and snorkelers of all abilities to enjoy Pulmo, although exercise care when exploring here, since this is open water, unprotected from wind, waves and currents. Winds often spring up in the afternoon, and heavy winds can restrict aquatic activities from January through mid-March for days at a time. Since the innermost coral heads can be found in shallow water immediately off the beach, snorkeling is excellent.

El Cantil, a site on the outermost rows of corals, lies less than a mile east of the beach, in about 45 ft. The only problem for photographers amid this profusion of life is deciding which lens to bring.

Pulmo is a National Marine Park. Spearfishing, foraging and shell collecting are not permitted. The northern boundary of the marine park is an east/west line 3.75 miles north of Cabo Pulmo, the southern an east/west line 0.5 mile south of the north shore of Cabo Frailes. The eastern boundary is on a north/south line 2.5 miles east of Cabo Pulmo. Information on current regulations can be obtained from one of the local dive operators.

To visit Pulmo, turn northeast on the paved road at KM 91+ on the Trans-peninsular, 57 miles south of La Paz. At KM 10+, turn southeast and set odometer. The pavement ends at mile 10.4, but the gravel road is well-graded. Arrive at Pulmo at mile 16.3. Three informal restaurants offer good meals and **Cabo Pulmo Beach Resort** has rental homes and bungalows. There are many spots where campers can spend the night and there is a launch ramp at Pulmo.

TOM HAIGHT

A hawkfish hides in the coral reef at Cabo Pulmo.

45 *Vencedor*

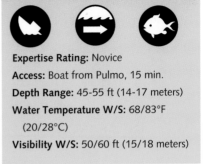

In 1980, the large Mexican fishing vessel *Vencedor* sank northeast of Cabo Pulmo. Today she is badly broken up, but with her great pile of machines, broken ribs and sections of hull all strewn across a sandy bottom, she is a favorite dive for those visiting Pulmo.

The *Vencedor* is the haunt of many of the species found on the coral reef, especially the pelagics. Because of the big fish and abundant coral life, this wreck is a favorite with photographers. The *Vencedor* is within the boundaries of the

Expertise Rating: Novice

Access: Boat from Pulmo, 15 min.

Depth Range: 45-55 ft (14-17 meters)

Water Temperature W/S: 68/83°F
   (20/28°C)

Visibility W/S: 50/60 ft (15/18 meters)

National Marine Park, so touch or take nothing.

Divers check out the partial remains of the *Vencedor*.

Colorful reef life abounds in the East Cape.

TOM HAIGHT

46 Los Frailes

Los Frailes is marked by rocky formations, thought by the locals to look like Catholic friars. Its bottom topography is also similar as it has a gently sloping sandy bottom, quickly plunging into a steep, rocky abyss. In a few places, small rivers of sand also course down its walls. Although there can be strong currents offshore, the shelter provided by the rocks keeps the tiny bay calm. Five miles south of Pulmo, the northern part of the bay falls into the National Marine Park boundaries. The nearby **Hotel Bahía los Frailes** has excellent accommodations.

Los Frailes is one of the few beach dives in Baja where really large pelagic fish can be seen very close to shore, including marlin and yellowfin tuna. The surrounding area is the best place in the world to see roosterfish, which have gray and silver bodies with two dark, curved stripes on

Expertise Rating: Intermediate
Access: Beach dive
Depth Range: Shallow-130 ft (40 meters)
Water Temperature W/S: 68/83°F
  (20/28°C)
Visibility W/S: 50/60 ft (15/18 meters)

their flanks. They get very large, up to 114 lbs. Their most noticeable feature underwater is their spectacular dorsal rays, which they erect when excited. Roosterfish are generally found on shallow reefs and sandy bottoms from the surf line out to very moderate depths, usually no more than 15 ft, especially where shallow rocky bottoms come up to meet sandy beaches.

TAMMY PELUSO

Spottail grunts appreciate the shelter provided by a wreck.

The Friendly Mantas

Found from Santa Barbara to Peru, Pacific manta rays are common in the Cortez up to the Midriff. They are black or dark-gray with a whip-like tail and twin horns projecting forward from their heads. The key to their uniqueness, however, is their flapping wings and immense size—they can be huge, spanning up to 25 ft across and weighing up to almost 4,000 lbs.

Baja's manta rays have had to fight some rather bad press right from the beginning, when Father Antonio Ascension observed in 1602, "One fish which is like nothing else grows [here]; it appears to be a mossy blanket extending to several unequal points. Its motion is scarcely perceptible, but when its prey is near it moves with great speed and enfolds and squeezes it. It is a very rare man who can save his life even though he is armed to strike out and defend himself."

Even the early Cortez pearl divers feared for their lives, but no manta has ever squeezed a diver. In fact mantas consume only plankton and small fishes. The only teeth they have is a tiny set on the lower jaw. Still, suspicion lingered on; in the 1966 Batman movie, Batman kept a spray can of "manta ray repellent" handy.

In 1980 a television crew anchored on El Bajo to film a movie about the schooling hammerhead sharks. A 16-ft manta came by, swimming slowly, with something obviously wrong. Divers found ropes tangled around the manta's left wing, which were embedded with a number of fish hooks. Another rope had cut deeply near the manta's eye. Sensing the divers wanted to help, the manta let them

TAMMY PELUSO

come close, cut off the rope and remove the hooks. When this was complete, the manta allowed one of the divers to climb on its back, taking him for a swooping, soaring ride. Returning the first diver, the fish gave the others a chance and if a diver dropped off, it would circle back and pick him up. It hung around the entire time the crew was on the seamount, offering rides to whomever wanted them.

From that point on, these once-fearsome creatures have been compared to puppy dogs wanting to play. Trips were offered to El Bajo to see the mantas, but in 1984, the fish became scarce. They returned unexpectedly during the summer of 1989 and there have been recent encounters at Cabo San Lucas. Recent regulations prohibit riding on the mantas, but friendly visits are still possible.

Los Cabos Area

Los Cabos, which includes the coastline between San José del Cabo and Cabo San Lucas, offers some of the best diving and snorkeling on the peninsula. These sites, combined with fine hotels and restaurants, a number of RV parks, a nearby international airport, mild and sunny weather, make Los Cabos an ideal location to spend a diving and snorkeling holiday. You'll also find lively night-life and numerous well-equipped dive shops offering trips, excursions and full rentals and sales. There are currently 10 dive operations in the Los Cabos area: **Amigos del Mar, Baja Dive Expeditions, Cabo Acuadeportes** (two locations), **J & R Baja Divers, Land's End Divers, Neptune Divers, Pacific Coast Adventures, Tío Sports** and **Underwater Diversions.** Boats can be launched at the Marina Cabo San Lucas ramp.

TAMMY PELUSO

The view of Neptune's Finger (*La Larga*) from Lover's Beach.

Los Cabos Area Dive Sites	Good Snorkeling	Novice	Intermediate	Advanced
47 Banco Gorda			✓	✓
48 Chileno	✓	✓	✓	✓
49 Santa María	✓	✓	✓	✓
50 Land's End		✓	✓	✓

47 Banco Gorda

Gorda is a seamount 8 miles off San José del Cabo. The great attraction here is the large marine life, found in such proliferation that Gorda is one of the premier dive sites in Baja. Whale sharks, mantas and striped marlin can be encountered and you can sometimes swim with the gray whales during their annual migration. At the bottom, you'll find black coral, gorgonians, sea fans and many species of benthic fish. A dive computer or watch, tables and depth gauge are essential at this site.

Expertise Rating: Intermediate

Access: Boat from Cabo San Lucas, 1½ hrs

Depth Range: 110-130 ft (34-40 meters)

Water Temperature W/S: 70/80°F (21/27°C)

Visibility W/S: 60/70 ft (18/21 meters)

All the dive shops in the Los Cabos area offer trips to Gorda. Because of the abundant marine life and good visibility, Gorda is an excellent location for wide-angle photography. However its depth limits bottom time, so shooting a 36-exposure roll is difficult. The low level of ambient light at the bottom can make passive focusing difficult, so a strobe with a modeling light is handy. None of the shops promotes Gorda as a snorkeling site, but your non-scuba friends could cruise around the dive boat in calm weather, looking for large fish in the water column.

A photographer gets a good shot of a whale shark.

TED RULISON

48 Chileno

Bahía Chileno has rocky reefs alternating with sandy areas. Because of its easy beach entry, minimal currents and surge, extensive shallow areas and dense colorful marine life, Chileno is an ideal location for novice divers and snorkelers. Advanced divers will also find numerous attractions in deeper water. Photographers, both wide-angle and macro, will enjoy the bay, and a night dive here is a special treat.

For reasons known only to themselves, beautiful gold- and blue-striped Panamic porkfish are more numerous at Chileno than at any other area in Baja waters. The small bay is also a rare place to view a medley of Panamic green morays, jewel morays, zebra morays and several species of tiger eel—all of which congregate at Chileno.

To get there, drive to KM 14+ on the Transpeninsular, 11 miles west of San José del Cabo. All local dive shops offer scuba and snorkeling excursions to Chileno and night dives are available.

Expertise Rating: Novice
Access: Beach dive
Depth Range: 10-60 ft (3-18 meters)
Water Temperature W/S: 70/80°F
 (21/27°C)
Visibility W/S: 50/60 ft (15/18 meters)

Helping Others

A number of fish and invertebrates make careers out of cleaning others. In the Cortez, the redhead goby, wide-banded cleaner goby and a half-dozen or so species of shrimp offer their services at cleaning stations, where customers assemble to be groomed. The cleaners advertise themselves in a variety of ways, hoping their often bright, unmistakable coloration convinces larger creatures that cleanliness is more important than an easy meal. Cleaners often enter the mouths of Panamic green morays and the gills of gigantic groupers, coming out again once a thorough cleaning job is done. The relationship is symbiotic (mutually beneficial): the cleaner gets a meal and the cleaned gets rid of parasites.

TAMMY PELUSO

For such beautiful creatures, Panamic porkfish have a rather pedestrian name.

TAMMY PELUSO

A wide-banded cleaner goby cleans a Panamic green moray.

All in Good Fin

Several divers were participating in a Land's End trip when two sea lions came by to play. One turned and seized a fin from one of the divers and raced off with it in his mouth. After a minute or two playing with the fin, the sea lion evidently grew tired of the game and let the fin go. The diver retrieved it, put it on, only to have the other sea lion rush in and pull it off. The fun finally ended and the diver got his fin back, in good shape except for a few tooth marks.

NEPTUNE DIVERS

Gee, guys, can't I play too?

49 Santa María

Caleta Santa María is a public beach, with easy beach access and fine diving on coral heads. The depths, conditions and marine life are very similar to Chileno. To get to the beach, turn south at KM 12+ on the Transpeninsular and drive 0.3 mile, park at the gate. The beach is an easy 5-minute walk. All local dive shops offer scuba and snorkeling excursions to Santa María and night dives are available.

Expertise Rating: Novice
Access: Beach dive
Depth Range: 10-60 ft (3-18 meters)
Water Temperature W/S: 70/80°F
   (21/27°C)
Visibility W/S: 50/60 ft (15/18 meters)

50 Land's End

Several tributaries of an enormous underwater canyon begin in the bay at Cabo San Lucas. Starting with a rather modest slope, the canyon descends at an average of 75% within a few hundred feet. It then levels off to a slope of 10%, which it maintains until the water is 6,000 ft deep. Granite walls tower over the bottom of the canyon and, at 5,400 ft, the walls are over 3,000 ft high. Were it on dry land, the topography would likely get rave reviews from tourists.

Expertise Rating: Novice
Access: Boat from Cabo, 10 min.
Depth Range: Shallow-130 ft (40 meters)
Water Temperature W/S: 70/80°F
   (21/27°C)
Visibility W/S: 50/60 ft (15/18 meters)

TAMMY PELUSO

Land's End is one of Baja's landmark sights.

The waters off the beaches out to Frailes (not to be confused with the Los Frailes just south of Pulmo) offer fine diving and no other important dive location in Baja is so easily accessible from a sizable town. There is much to see. The narrow strip of land leading out to Frailes is overtopped by waves during storms, carrying sand into the bay. Long rivers of excess sand from the beach flow down the tributaries of the canyon, forming sandfalls when they reach the cliffs. The sand falls begin at about 90 ft and continue far past the safe scuba limit.

Divers have coined names for the various locations, such as the Cabo San Lucas Canyon Wall, the Sand Falls, Anegada (Pelican Rock), Neptune's Finger (a tall rock spire), Lover's Beach and The Point.

Rocky areas are covered with lush growths of corals and gorgonians, and there are many species of fish to be seen. There is an old shipwreck just west of the last rock to the south, which is sometimes the haunt of very large groupers. Be careful when diving here, as fishing boats often troll by, ignoring the diver's flag. Fishing lures often snag the wreck, leaving small treasures to be collected by divers.

Land's End has areas suitable for the full range of divers and snorkelers, from Novice to Advanced. Stay at depths suitable to your ability and watch your gauge because it can get deep. The Sand Falls should be visited only by qualified divers with deep water experience. Touch nothing and take nothing, for the bay is a National Marine Sanctuary.

Islas de Revillagigedo Dive Sites

Despite the romantic idea that its majestic rock formations mark "Land's End," there is actually a group of islands south of Cabo San Lucas. The Revillagigedo Islands—also known informally as the Socorro Islands—include San Benedicto, Socorro and Clarión, plus a tiny islet, Roca Partida. The islands are widely spread apart; Benedicto and Clarión lie 277 nautical miles (513 km) away from each other. All are small—the largest, Socorro, is only about 9 by 11 miles (15 by 18 km) and the smallest, Partida, is a mere 50 by 100 yards (46 by 91 meters), the last remnants of the vent plug of a very old volcano. The islands are owned by Mexico and are uninhabited, with the exception of a small naval base on Socorro. The surrounding waters are so prolific that long-range sportfishing boats frequently make the 1,730-mile (2,784 km) round trip from San Diego. Revillagigedos is pronounced ray-veeh-yah-hee-**hay**-does (it gets easier with practice).

In recent years, Benedicto, 220 nautical miles (400 km) south of Cabo San Lucas and Socorro, 33 nautical miles (61.2 km) south of Benedicto, have become major destinations for well-heeled divers. The underwater landscape is as stark, dramatic and varied as the topside landscape, with giant boulders, rocky, coral-covered slopes, lonely pinnacles and rippled flows of lava.

The underwater topography surrounding Isla Socorro is as rugged as the island itself.

The Rumbling Revillagigedos

All four islands in the Revillagigedos are volcanic in origin. Benedicto had such a violent eruption in 1952 that the crew of the tuna clipper *Challenger* stood in awe of the huge 10,000-ft cloud of dark volcanic ash and in trepidation of the shower of glowing volcanic bombs. Perhaps unknown to them, the crew had witnessed the birth of Volcán Barceno.

KENNETH J HOWARD

Due to vocanic activity and erosion, San Benedicto's profile continually changes.

The topside flora and fauna of the islands are unique, comprised of numerous endemic (found only in one area on earth) species. Unfortunately, introduced herbivores and predators are wreaking havoc on the islands, especially on Socorro, where sheep are destroying the delicate habitat. Increased erosion is depositing immense amounts of materials in the waters surrounding Socorro, bringing unhappy prospects for the long-term health of the underwater environment.

Sighting 30 or 40 species in a day of diving would not be unusual. You can see sought-after game fish like dorado, yellowfin tuna, wahoo and marlin. The islands are home to many species that are not likely to be seen in the Cortez: blue-spotted surgeonfish, redtail triggerfish, Socorro chub, Socorro crown-of-thorns, Socorro wrasse, trumpetfish.

In spite of the relative isolation of the islands from the peninsula, a number of species are shared including: bluefin trevally, burrito grunt, glasseye, green jack, guineafowl puffer, leather bass, longnose butterflyfish, Moorish idols, plain cardinalfish, scissortail damselfish, tiger reef eel and vagabond filefish. The sunset wrasse, found in limited numbers in the Cape region, is common at the Revillagigedos.

Despite these varied riches, the main attraction of the islands is the very large Pacific manta rays. These great fish are unafraid of divers, to the point that their curiosity gets the best of them and they will often come very, very close. One jubilant diver recently said, "Quite honestly, nothing compares with the experience of having a manta ray cruise up to you, stop inches away and look you square in the eye. It just doesn't get any better." In addition to the mantas, divers may encounter other "big fellows" that may not be quite so tranquil including the Galapagos, scalloped hammerhead, silvertip, tiger and silky sharks. A trip to the islands may be an unsettling experience to a few, but it will be a life-long, world-class memory for all.

Currents occasionally reach two knots to the south and, since the Revillagigedos are unprotected oceanic islands, the swell can be large and the surge on north shores can be heavy. Because of this and the presence of very large animals—some of which may look threatening and purposeful—the learning curve is very steep for divers and snorkelers, no matter what their experience level.

Only one vessel home-ported in Baja California makes trips to the Revillagigedos, the *Solmar V*, which offers 9-day excursions from November through May. The boat visits Socorro, San Benedicto and Partida, as well as occasional 11-day trips to Clarión. Roca Partida is so small that the entire islet is considered a single site; divers can circumnavigate it on a single tank.

The islands are a "Protected Biosphere," so check with Amigos del Mar, which manages diving operations on the *Solmar V*, about current regulations.

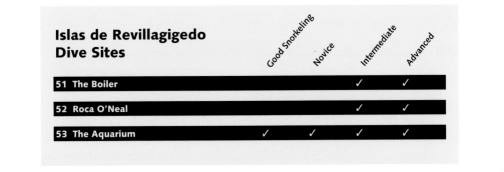

Islas de Revillagigedo Dive Sites	Good Snorkeling	Novice	Intermediate	Advanced
51 The Boiler			✓	✓
52 Roca O'Neal			✓	✓
53 The Aquarium	✓	✓	✓	✓

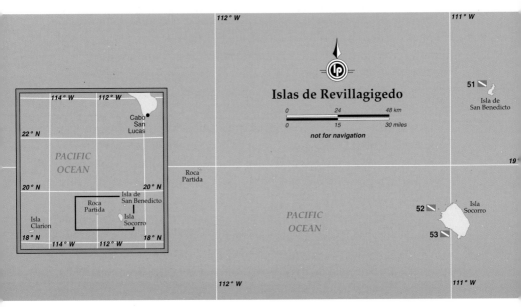

51 The Boiler

Located just west of Benedicto's north end, the steep walls of this small, flat-topped seamount drop to a sandy bottom at 140 ft, and are packed with colorful life. The stars of this underwater show are the Pacific mantas rays. They may be attracted to the site by cleaner fish: the mantas hang virtually motionless while cleanerfish remove parasites and debris from their bodies. Mantas often stop in the line of regulator bubbles and although it varies, it is not unusual to have six or seven mantas spend part of a day playing with you.

The seamount is also home to large numbers of Clarion angelfish. Like their more common cousins, the Cortez angelfish and the king angelfish, juvenile Clarion angelfish have very different coloration from adults, so much that they often get mistaken for a separate species. Adult Clarion angelfish have an orange body, while the young are yellow, with a number of vertical blue stripes on their flanks. Their love-life is confusing, at least to humans: they are protogynous hermaphrodites, beginning their lives as females and later changing to males. Males form harems of up to five females and aggressively chase off any would-be suitors. The species has been seen carrying out cleanerfish duties on Pacific manta rays.

Expertise Rating: Intermediate

Access: Boat from Cabo, 22 hrs

Depth Range: 20-130 ft (6-40 meters)

Water Temperature W/S: 70/82°F (21/28°C)

Visibility W/S: 60/70 ft (18/21 meters)

Clarion angelfish swim through The Boiler.

The Revillagigedos are excellent for close encounters with Pacific manta rays.

52 Roca O'Neal

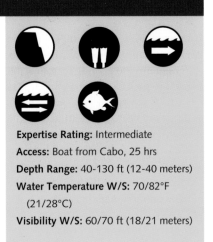

It is possible to see the entire range of the region's marine life at O'Neal Rock, located off Socorro's western side. Here you can see tiger sharks, scalloped hammerheads, silky, Galapagos and silver-tip sharks and manta rays. You may see what appears to be an ordinary California spiny lobster, except that the bases of its antennas are bright blue, identifying it as the Socorro spiny lobster. Despite its name, it is not a Socorro endemic—it is also found in the Red Sea, the Indian Ocean and off South Africa. The lobsters here are enormous and it is not uncommon to see them prowling around, even at mid-day. Panamic green morays seem to be everywhere, some lying out of their caves and crevices during the day, a most un-moraylike behavior. Schools of hammerheads are occasionally seen.

A flat spot at about 40 ft features interesting ledges and crevices brimming with

Expertise Rating: Intermediate
Access: Boat from Cabo, 25 hrs
Depth Range: 40-130 ft (12-40 meters)
Water Temperature W/S: 70/82°F (21/28°C)
Visibility W/S: 60/70 ft (18/21 meters)

invertebrates. One of the most scenic spots is a wall at about 100 ft, where a huge rock arch provides a great backdrop for photos. Large swells sometimes break on the rock and surge can easily exceed 5 ft, so stay well away from the rock until you're in deep water.

53 The Aquarium

This unique snorkel site on Socorro's southwest side is a large, shallow pool carpeted with colorful corals and home to immense populations of juvenile fish and invertebrates. A good dive site, sometimes called northwesterlies, The Outer Aquarium, is located immediately offshore, where divers will find large coral heads and abundant marine life in 30 to 60 ft. During the prevailing northwesterlies, The Aquarium is the most protected snorkeling site in the region.

A catalog of the many creatures found in the pool and the offshore site would be many pages long, but would include blue-spotted surgeonfish, branching

Expertise Rating: Novice
Access: Boat from Cabo, 25 hrs
Depth Range: 5-15 ft (2-5 meters)
Temperature W/S: 70/82°F (21/28°C)
Visibility W/S: 40/50 ft (12/15 meters)

stony coral, brown urchin, Clarion angelfish, Clarion damselfish, Socorro spiny lobster, redtail triggerfish, Socorro chub, Socorro crown-of-thorns, tiger reef eel, tube worm, green wrasse,

A diver encounters burrito grunts and several other species
of fish under a ledge lined with sea fans.

sunset wrasse and Socorro wrasse. In the pool, miniature lobsters, several inches long, are brave enough to wander openly during the day, but their life-span would be measured in minutes should they decide to leave.

Marine Life

JERRY MARTIN

The marine life off Baja's Pacific shores offers few surprises. There is a fairly orderly transition from cool-water to warm-water species, as might be expected along a coast having a limited number of habitats and a south-bound current offshore. The Cortez, however, is an entirely different story. Scientists have identified 132 families, 431 genera, and over 800 species of marine life in Cortez waters; 17% of the species are endemic, or native to the Cortez. Excluding deep-sea fishes, 92% have tropical affinities, which seems remarkable, since only the most southern 50 miles (80 km) of the peninsula lies south of the Tropic of Cancer.

This chapter provides photographs of 36 common and interesting marine animals found in Baja waters and at the Islas de Revillagigedo, followed by photographs and information on a number of hazardous marine creatures.

Vertebrates

barberfish
Johnrandallia nigrirostris

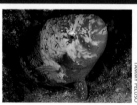

bicolor parrotfish
Scarus rubroviolaceus

blue-and-gold snapper
Lutjanus viridis

California needlefish
Strongylura exilis

Clarion angelfish
Holacanthus clarionensis

Cortez damselfish
Stegastes rectifraenum

130

garibaldi
Hypsypops rubicundus

guineafowl puffer
Arothron meleagris

leopard grouper
Mycteroperca rosacea

longnose butterflyfish
Forcipiger flavissimus

jewel moray
Muraena lentiginosa

Mexican barracuda
Sphyraena lucasana

Mexican hogfish
Bodianus diplotaenia

Moorish idol
Zanclus cornutus

Pacific seahorse
Hippocampus ingens

Panamic porkfish
Anisotremus taeniatus

Panamic sergeant major
Abudefduf troschelii

Panamic soldierfish
Myripristis leiognathos

redtail triggerfish
Xanthichthys mento

yellowtail surgeonfish
Prionurus punctatus

Pacific manta ray
Manta hamilitoni

California sea lion
Zalophus californianus

scalloped hammerhead shark
Sphyrna lewini

whale shark
Rhincodon typus

Invertebrates

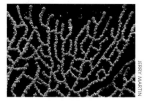
California spiny lobster
Panulirus interruptus

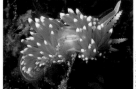
blue-striped sea slug
Tambja eliora

elegant hermit crab
Aniculus elegans

gorgonian
Suborder: *Holaxonia*

Hermissenda nudibranch
Hermissenda crassicornis

orange cup coral
Tubastraea coccinea

purplelip rock oyster
Spondylus calcifer

Rathburn's sea star
Rathbunaster californicus

red anemone
Corynactis californica

tan sea star
Phataria unifascialis

tidepool shrimp
Palaemon ritteri

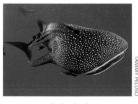
sulfur sponge
Aplysina fistularis

Hazardous Marine Life

The greatest dangers facing Baja divers and snorkelers are largely self-inflicted and easily avoidable. Just as there are bears, bees and poison ivy in the forest, the ocean has its share of natural hazards. Following a few precautions will greatly reduce your chance of an unhappy encounter:

- Wear a full wetsuit or Lycra skin, which will minimize the amount of exposed skin.
- Maintain neutral buoyancy, or better yet, a bit of positive buoyancy.
- Do not step on, kick, or touch anything.
- Never feed or tease any marine animal.

Stinging Hydroids

Class: Hydrozoa Feather- or fern-like "branches" make many species of hydroids look like plants, but they are actually colonies of polyps growing on a common stalk. They convey no hint of menace, but some species possess stinging cells called nematocysts (capsules containing tiny needles armed with a toxin), which can be triggered by touch or chemical stimulus. The typical reaction to a hydroid encounter is a mild stinging sensation, soon followed by a rash. Most divers and snorkelers consider hydroid stings to be just a minor nuisance. Weakness, headache, nausea, vomiting, muscle spasm, fever, pallor, rapid or irregular heartbeat and/or breathing difficulties may develop in rare cases.

WALT PETERSON

In the Cortez, stinging hydroids are found from the Midriff area to the Cape.

Jellyfish

Class Scyphozoa In their adult (medusal) phase, jellyfish are gelatinous, translucent creatures, often mushroom-shaped with trailing tentacles. They range in size from a grain of rice to over 8 ft in diameter. Some species use rhythmic contractions to expel water, allowing them to move forward by jet propulsion, while others simply drift with the currents. They use the nematocysts in their tentacles for defense and to capture plankton, fish, and other jellyfish. Sting symptoms range from moderate pain and a rash to blistering, cramps, shock, paralysis, and heart failure.

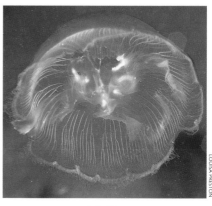

LOUISA PRESTON

Jellyfish

Man-o-War

Physalia sp. Although it may appear to be a jellyfish, the man-o-war is actually a member of the Class Hydrozoa and cousin to the plant-like hydroids described above. The man-o-war is found at the surface, recognizable by its purplish, translucent pouch of gas and long, flowing tentacles. Its tentacles, which can reach 50 ft or more in length, are heavily armed with nematocysts, which are used to sting prey and for defense. Carried by the winds, tides, and currents, they are often cast ashore. Beached man-o-wars are still hazardous, even weeks after they've dried out and appear dead. Divers and snorkelers should be careful on entering the water and when surfacing. Symptoms range from a mild itch to intense pain, blistering, skin discoloration, shock, breathing difficulties and unconsciousness. Man-o-war stings can be fatal.

TIM ROCK

Beached, dead-looking man-o-wars can still be hazardous.

Sea Stars

Class: Asteroidea Sea stars, every child's "starfish," are easily recognized and most are harmless. However, a few species can be hazardous to humans. With ten or more short "arms," the sinister-looking **Panamic crown-of-thorns** is found in the Southern Cortez and Cape regions and south to Peru. A second, closely related species is the **Socorro crown-of-thorns**, found at the Revillagigedos, and a third inhabits the Indo-Pacific region to the west, where it is notorious for the damage it does

The spines of the Panamic crown-of-thorns are sharp and venomous.

to coral reefs. All three may be the same species; marine biologists are uncertain. Their sharp spines contain venom and break off easily, leaving the unwary diver with puncture wounds, redness, swelling and a good deal of pain. Spine fragments are sometimes visible in the wound. Other species of sea stars in Baja waters are also armed with spines, some rounded and blunt, others sharp and needle-like.

Sea Urchins

Class: Echinoidea Although they vary in coloration and size, with spines ranging from blunt to needle-sharp, sea urchins are not hard to identify; just look for a "sea-going pincushion." With numerous sharp, toxic spines—up to 5-inches long in some species—they present a formidable defense that few divers and snorkelers will choose to challenge. However, sea urchin

Accidentally stepping on a crowned urchin would be an experience long-remembered.

wounds are one of the more common injuries in Baja waters, often suffered in areas of heavy surge or upon entry or exit from the water. Hands, knees, and feet are the most commonly injured areas. The symptoms include intense pain, numbness, and occasionally paralysis, faintness and nausea.

Scorpionfish

Family: Scorpaenidae Because scorpionfish inhabit relatively shallow water, are well camouflaged and don't flee from approaching divers, encounters with them are possible at almost any dive site described in this book. They are difficult to see, but once seen and recognized, they prove to be more common than might be expected. Look for a "blob," probably mot-

The scorpionfish's camouflage makes it difficult to spot.

tled red and brown, 6 to 18 inches long, with a large, spiny head and numerous ragged skin flaps. They are usually seen in rocky crevices during the day, occasionally in sandy areas, but are also seen free-swimming at night. The venomous spines on their backs make nasty puncture wounds, usually on a hand or foot. Such wounds do not bleed much but are painful and long-lasting, sometimes becoming infected by bacteria carried into the wound by the spines. Wounds can be identified by intense pain, a puncture in the skin and a blue tinge to the surrounding skin.

Rays

Families: Myliobatidiae, Gymnuridae & Dasyatididae Some species of rays are well-armed: their whip-like tails have a hard, sharp spine equipped with serrations and venom glands. The spine is covered with a sheath, which tends to remain in the wound. Most stingrays are encountered in sandy or silty areas in shallow water, where they lie on the bottom or bury themselves. Often only the eyes, gill slits, and tail are visible. Four species of ray commonly encountered by divers in Baja have spines: the diamond, round, California butterfly and bat ray. A ray wound can be identified by the spine or fragments of the sheath in the skin, surrounded by swollen, bleeding tissue. The victim may be in great pain and nauseated to the point of throwing up and may experience cramps or paralysis.

WALT PETERSON

Bullseye electric rays are not too common, which is fortunate for divers—stepping on one can be a shocking experience.

The silky shark is abundant, large, pelagic and can be somewhat aggressive.

Sharks

Families: Carcharhinidae, Sphyrnidae & Lamnidae Because of sharks' sinister appearance and "bad press" in the media, most people regard them as the most aggressive and dangerous species in the oceans. Knowledgeable people know this to be untrue. Many species are shy, and some are in decline worldwide due to human activities, such as over-fishing and pollution. Still, there are occasional attacks. About 25 species world-wide are considered dangerous. In Baja waters these include: the bonito, narrowtooth, bull, oceanic whitetip, dusky, tiger, blue, smooth hammerhead and great white. Other than hammerheads with their distinctive head shape, shark identification isn't always easy. It is prudent to consider all large sharks potentially dangerous (some of the smaller ones can also bite or have spines). The best policy is avoidance; don't bother them and they're a lot less likely to bother you.

Other Potential Hazards

Other potentially hazardous creatures include: some sponges and corals (toxins produce a mild, itchy rash); surgeonfish (sharp spines near tail); cone shells (some possess stingers); bristle worms (tiny but painful bristles that enter the skin); octopus (they can bite); Panamic moray eels (very sharp teeth and powerful jaws); and bullseye electric rays (can produce an electric shock). However, injuries by this group are exceedingly rare.

Several species of octopus live in Baja waters. Some can bite.

Basic First Aid Procedures

The measures described below are basic first aid using commonly available materials and equipment, and are not a substitute for medical attention. The seriousness of an encounter with a hazardous marine animal depends not only on the nature of the animal but on the location of the wound—a bite, spine or sting near the eyes is a very different thing than one to a calloused heel.

1. Immediately, in the water if possible, insure that the victim is breathing. If not, make sure the airway is clear and begin mouth-to-mouth resuscitation. Remove the victim from the water as quickly as possible, check for breathing and heartbeat, begin CPR if necessary.

2. To minimize shock, place the victim in a head-down position; minimize blood loss by applying pressure and/or a tourniquet and elevate the limb involved.

3. Try to remove spiracles, spines, or bristles with tweezers or adhesive tape, but leave any that are deeply embedded (in joints, near eyes, or near major blood vessels) for surgical removal later. Wash the area with sterile (boiled) water. If a sponge is thought to be involved, soak the area with vinegar diluted with an equal volume of sterile water. Venom and pain may be reduced by heating the afflicted area with warm water or a hot hair drier.

4. If a creature with nematocysts was involved, the sting should be washed out with sea water. (Do not use fresh water, as nematocysts will trigger in defense of something "unnatural" to them; fresh water may in fact result in additional stings.) Flood the area with diluted vinegar and remove any visible nematocysts with a pair of tweezers. Apply shaving cream to the site, and carefully scrape it with a razor or knife. Flood the area again with diluted vinegar, followed by several teaspoons of baking soda (sodium bicarbonate) dissolved in sterile water. Make sure nematocysts are not spread to other areas—especially the eyes—or other people.

5. Apply a topical antibiotic such as bacitracin or neomycin if available. Place a sterile dressing over the wound—a section cut from a clean cotton T-shirt or wash-cloth, boiled and then dried will do fine—and secure it with tape or string.

Diving
Conservation
& Awareness

TAMMY PELUSO

Increased commercial fishing, diving and other human activities are placing immense pressure on the marine animals in Baja waters. Commercial divers have virtually wiped out the "flying clams" of Bahía de los Ángeles and the scallops of Bahía Concepción, and are now taking large numbers of sea urchins and sea cucumbers for sale to Japan.

Mexico has responded in a number of ways. Marine parks and reserves of various categories have been established at Loreto, Cabo San Lucas, Pulmo Reef and the Revillagigedos. There has been talk of establishing others, including one at Bahía de los Ángeles. In these parks and reserves, divers and snorkelers are prohibited from taking or molesting any form of marine life, and there are regulations concerning human interaction with marine life. The Revillagigedos are the most tightly regulated and permits to enter are required (obtained by the dive operator, not individual divers).

As is so often the case in Mexico, regulations concerning these parks and reserves are often poorly drafted and subject to a host of interpretations. However well-intentioned, these measures have little or no funding attached, and with a rapidly expanding

Evaluating Dive Operators' Conservation Efforts

While out on the water, note what actions the dive operation, boat operator and divemaster are taking to protect the environment. There should be permanent anchoring buoys at all regularly visited sites. The boat speed should be greatly reduced in shallow areas, as much for the safety of the passengers as the critters below.

During the briefing does the divemaster address conservation matters? Once in the water, are people who allow their consoles to drag on the bottom, crashing against corals and sea fans, gently but firmly advised otherwise?

At the end of a trip, when it comes to critiques and tips, consider conservation matters in addition to such things as the quality of the box lunch or the personality of the divemaster.

population that must be fed and employed, Mexico's conservation laws are widely ignored. If you plan to dive or snorkel in one of the parks or reserves, obtain current information from your dive operator or from the office of the Secretary of Tourism in the appropriate state.

You can help in reversing the continuing decline in the underwater ecosystem in a numbers of ways. In dealing with travel agents, hotels and resorts, let it be known that you are a diver or snorkeler coming to see the area's marine creatures, and that conservation will be a central consideration in your choices. In selecting dive operations, inquire about their conservation policies. While out on the water, note what actions the dive operation, boat operator and divemaster have taken to protect the environment.

Responsible Diving

The popularity of diving is placing immense pressure on many sites. Please consider the following tips when diving, and help to preserve the ecology and beauty of the reefs:

1. Do not use anchors on the reef, and take care not to ground boats on coral. Encourage dive operators and regulatory bodies to establish permanent moorings at popular dive sites.

2. Avoid touching living marine organisms with your body or dragging equipment across the reef. Polyps can be damaged by even the gentlest contact. Never stand on corals, even if they look solid and robust. If you must hold onto the reef, touch only exposed rock or dead coral. If you accidentally kick something, stop kicking and add a little air to your BC to lift yourself away.

A snorkeler checks out a young whale shark and its passengers.

3. Be conscious of your fins, for their surge can damage delicate organisms. Avoid treading water in shallow areas; settling sand or silt can easily smother the delicate marine life. A properly weighted diver should not have to tread water.

4. Practice proper buoyancy control. Major damage can be done by divers descending too fast and colliding with the reef. Make sure you are correctly weighted and that your weight belt is positioned so that you stay horizontal.

5. Underwater photographers often become so wrapped up locating subjects, adjusting f-stops, speed and strobes that they are unaware of the damage they do to their surroundings. Use special care to keep a stable, horizontal position with a tiny bit of positive buoyancy. If you are using extension tubes or a close-up outfit, remember that your framer can do considerable damage to your subject.

6. Resist the temptation to collect or buy corals or shells. Aside from the ecological damage, taking home marine souvenirs depletes the beauty of a site and spoils others' enjoyment. The same goes for marine archaeological sites (mainly shipwrecks). Respect their integrity; some sites are even protected from looting by law.

7. Ensure that you take home all your trash and any litter you may find as well. Plastics in particular are a serious threat to marine life. Turtles can mistake plastic for jellyfish and eat it.

8. Resist the temptation to feed fish. You may disturb their normal eating habits, encourage aggressive behavior or feed them food that is detrimental to their health.

9. Minimize your disturbance of marine animals. Don't ride on the backs of turtles or manta rays, as this can cause them great anxiety.

Diving & Environmental Organizations

A growing number of groups are actively promoting responsible diving practices, publicizing potential marine threats, and lobbying for better policies. Contact the following organizations for more information.

CEDAM International
☎ 914-271-5365
www.cedam.org
cedamint@aol.com

Cortez Conservation Club
☎ 011-52-112-16120
www.cortezclub.com/conserva.htm

Cousteau Society
☎ 757-523-9335
www.cousteau.org
cousteau@infi.net

Project AWARE Foundation
☎ 714-540-0251
www.padi.com/aware/default.htm
kirstinv@padi.com

SeaWeb
www.seaweb.org
seaweb@seaweb.org

Listings

Making Telephone Calls

Making a direct-dial call from the U.S. or Canada to a location in Baja is simple. First, dial 011(for international access), then the country code, which for Mexico is 52, and then the area code. All area codes in Baja have 3 digits, except for Ensenada, Mexicali and Tijuana, which have 2-digits, 61, 65 and 66 respectively. Finally, dial the local number, which has 5 digits, except the three cities just named, which have 6.

Accommodations

The resorts and hotels listed below cater specifically to divers and snorkelers and have an on-the-premises dive operation or one in the immediate vicinity, and/or operate live-aboard dive vessels. Virtually all resorts and hotels catering to tourists in the Southern Cortez and Cape regions can provide snorkeling gear for guests and make arrangements for scuba diving. Contact information for the affiliated dive operator is given in the "Dive Services" listing.

Baja Outpost
Loreto
Affiliated Dive Operation:
Baja Outpost

Casa Miramar
East Cape
Affiliated Dive Operation:
Baja Dive Adventures

Club Hotel Cantamar
La Paz
Affiliated Dive Operation:
Baja Diving & Service

Hotel Hacienda
Cabo San Lucas

Affiliated Dive Operation:
Cabo Acuadeportes

Hotel Solmar
Cabo San Lucas
Affiliated Dive Operation:
Cabo Resort Reservations

La Concha Beach Resort
La Paz
Affiliated Dive Operation:
Cortez Club

San Francisquito Resort
Bahía San Francisquito
Affiliated Dive Operation:
San Francisquito

Dining

There are hundreds of restaurants in Baja California at every price level and just about every specialty. The following, representing a range of prices and different specialties, are among the best:

Ensenada

El Rey Sol is an excellent French restaurant, opened in 1947 by a woman trained at the Cordon Bleu School of Cooking in France. Its menu includes such dishes as

Escargot de Bourguignon, Duck à l'Orange, steaks and seafood. With carpeted floors, carved cane-backed chairs and Chopin played on the piano, it has all the ambiance you could possibly want. While no one comes here to save money or calories, the meals are not unduly expensive by standards north of the border. It is located on Av. Lopéz Mateos at its intersection with Av. Blancarte.

San Quintín

Gaston's Cannery Restaurant serves seafood, including fish, shrimp, crab, oysters and lobster, as well as steaks and Mexican items. The fish cannery motif in the restaurant and the adjoining **Old Mill Saloon** creates a fine ambiance complemented by a fireplace, mariachi music and rustic furniture. To get to the restaurant, turn west on the graded dirt road at KM 1 in San Quintín, opposite a large electrical station and drive about 3 miles (5 km).

Guerrero Negro

La Espinita Restaurant serves Mexican and seafood dishes. The place is clean and the food and hospitality get rave reviews from travelers. It is located at KM 127+ on the Transpeninsular Highway, just north of Guerrero Negro. The **Malarrimo Restaurant** is popular, especially with seafood-eaters; try the breaded pismos, or the bay scallops sautéed in butter, garlic and wine. The restaurant is located on the right as you enter town.

Santa Rosalía

The beautiful **Hotel Frances** was built back when Santa Rosalía was a world-class copper mining town, its harbor crowded with great sailing ships from around the world. It has been restored with wide verandahs, polished wooden floors and ceilings. It is certainly the most unusual hotel in Baja. The restaurant serves seafood, chicken, beef and Mexican cuisine. To find it, turn west into the center of town from the Transpeninsular and watch for an unusual church on your right (it is made of cast iron, and was designed by Alexandre Gustave Eiffel, of tower fame). Turn right just before the church and once on top of the mesa, turn right.

Mulegé

The service is slow at **Restaurant el Candil**, but the food—including steaks, chicken, Mexican and seafood—is inexpensive and well-prepared. There is usually a guitarist to liven things up. El Candil is located on Av. Zaragoza, just south of Av. Gral. Martínez (the main drag). The restaurant at the **Hotel Serenidad** is the scene of legendary Mexican fiesta banquets on Wednesdays—complete with mariachis. Also note the Saturday night pig feed. The hotel is off the Transpeninsular east of the bridge—watch for the sign.

La Paz

Restaurant Kiwi is decorated with a beautiful design worked into the floor with colored tile, and imaginative wall hangings. There is an extensive menu and an outdoor dining area looking out over the beach and harbor. It is located on Av. Abasolo (the main drag, paralleling the waterfront) at Av. 5 de Mayo. **Restaurant Adriana**, on the beach near Av. Hidalgo, serves excellent fish dinners, nicely seasoned with garlic, at reasonable prices. **Restaurant Bismark** specializes in lobster, abalone, *carne asada*, deep-fried red snapper and *cochinita pibil*, a roast pork dish. It is located near the corner of Degollado and Altamirano.

San José del Cabo

The specialty of the house at the thatched-roofed **Iguana Restaurant & Bar** is seafood, but the New York steak is also excellent. It is located on Av. Mijares in the downtown area.

Cabo San Lucas

Fisherman's Pescadores serves good American-style breakfasts at modest prices. It is located on Av. Hidalgo in the downtown area. The **Giggling Marlin** serves good burgers, beer, mixed drinks, with a heavy dose of ersatz funk. It is located at Blvd. Marina and Matamoros. **El Galeón**, located south of the inner harbor area, is the most expensive restaurant in town, serving steaks and seafood, often accompanied by live music.

Tourist Services

Baja Bush Pilots
1255 West Baseline Road, Suite 138,
Mesa, Arizona 85202
☎ 602-730-3250 fax: 02-730-3251
Jack@bajabush.com

Cabo Resort Reservations
Box 383, Pacific Palisades, CA 90272
☎ 310-459-9861 fax: 310-454-1686
Toll-free ☎ 800-334-3349
caboresort@aol.com
Handles reservations for Amigos del Mar,
the Hotel Solmar, and the *Solmar V.*

California Baja Rent-A-Car
9245 Jamacha Blvd., Spring Valley, CA 91977
☎ 619-470-7368 fax: 619-479-2004
Toll-free ☎ 888-470-7368
info@cabaja.com
www.cabaja.com

Cruise America
11 West Hampton Ave., Mesa, AZ 85210
☎ 602-464-7300 fax: 602-464-7302
Toll-free ☎ 800-327-7799
travel@cruisemamerica.com
www.cruiseamerica .com

Discover Baja Travel Club
3089 Clairemont Dr., San Diego, CA 92117
☎ 619-275-4225 fax: 619-275-1836
Toll-free ☎ 800-727-2252
discovbaja@aol.com
www.discoverbaja.com

El Monte RV Rentals & Sales
12818 Firestone Blvd.
Santa Fe Springs, CA 90670
☎ 562 404-9300 fax: 562 909-8008
Toll-free ☎ 800 367-3687
reservations@elmonte.com
(within the U.S.)
international@elmonte.com
(outside the U.S.)
www.elmonte.com

Mexico Ministry of the Environment, Natural Resources, & Fisheries
2550 Fifth Avenue, Suite 101,
San Diego, CA 92103-6622
☎ 619-233-6956
fax: 619-233-0344

United States Customs Service
Box 7407, Washington, DC 20044
☎ 202-566-8195
www.customs.ustreas.gov

Vagabundos del Mar Boat & Travel Club
190 Main St., Rio Vista, CA 94571
☎ 707-374-5511 fax: 707-374-6843
Toll-free ☎ 800-474-2252
vags@compuserve.com
ourworld.compuserve.com/homepages/vags

Consulates

Canadian Consulate
German Gedovius 10411-101
Condominio del Parque
Tijuana, BC, México
☎ 66-840461 fax: 66-880301
rencinas@bbs.cincos.net

United States Consular Agency
Blvd. Marina y Calle de Cerro
Cabo San Lucas, BCS, México
☎/fax: 114-33566

United States Consulate General
Av. Tapachula 96,
Col. Hipódromo
Tijuana, BC, México
☎ 66-817400 fax: 66-818016
or
Box 439039, San Ysidro,
CA 92143
☎ 619-585-2350 (24-hour answering service)

Tourism Offices

State Secretary of Tourism of Baja California [Norte]
Edificio Centro de Gobierno, Blvd. Lázaro Cárdenas 1477
Ensenada, BC, México
☎ 011-52-61-723022 fax: 011-52-61-723081

Av. Mar de Cortez y Calle Manzanillo 300,
San Felipe, BC, México
☎/fax: 011-52-657-71155

Callejon Libertad 1305, Tecate, BC, México
☎/fax: 011-52-665-41095

State Secretary of Tourism of Baja California Sur
KM 5½, Carretera Transpeninsular (FIDEPAZ)
Apdo. Postal 419, La Paz, BCS, México
☎ 011-52-112-40100 fax: 011-52-112-40722
turismo@lapaz.cromwell.com.mx

Dive Services

Most Baja dive operators offer night dives, certification and specialty courses. Virtually all accept referrals and have resort and snorkeling courses available. See the previous section for direct-dialing instructions. Toll-free numbers can be reached from most U.S. and Canadian cities. Local driving directions are provided for operators without street addresses, either here or in the dive site descriptions earlier in the book.

Northern Pacific Region

Almar Dive Shop

Av. Macheros 149, Ensenada, BC, México
☎ 617-83013
Sales: Basic equipment, small parts
Rentals: None

Air: One compressor on premises
Credit cards: None
Comments: No boats or trips; small shop caters mainly to Mexican commercial divers

Horizon Charters

4178 Lochlomond Street,
San Diego, CA 92111, U.S.
☎ 619-277-7823 fax: 619-560-6811
divesd@aol.com
www.earthwindow.com/horizon
Sales: None Rentals: Tanks and weights
Air: On-board compressor
Credit cards: Visa, MasterCard

Boats: *Ocean Odyssey*, 85 ft long, 25-ft beam, watermakers, complete electronics and safety equipment, on-board compressors, swim platforms, underwater recall system, 35 passengers
Trips: Day-trips to Coronados & Pacific Coast sites from San Diego
Courses: None
Comments: Also operates the live-aboard *Horizon*

La Bufadora Dive

Mail: Dale Erwin, Apdo. Postal 102, Maneadero, BC, México
☎ 615-42092 fax: None
www.labufadora.com
Sales: None Rentals: Full
Air: One compressor on premises
Credit cards: None

Boats: 22-ft pangas with 40 h.p. outboard engines
Trips: All local sites Courses: None
Comments: Drive to Maneadero, 8.6 miles south of Ensenada on the Transpeninsular.Turn west on the road to Punta Banda and set odometer. The road continues until mile 13, at La Bufadora. Look for the dive flag. Accommodations are available

Lois Ann Dive Charters

5867 Lord Cecil Street, San Diego,
CA 92122, U.S.
☎ 619-450-4478 fax: 619-453-6306
Toll-free ☎ 800-201-4381
lois@loisann.com
www.loisann.com
Sales: None Rentals: Full except wet suits
Air: 4,000 psi on-board compressor; Nitrox fills

Credit cards: All major cards, Discover
Boats: *Lois Ann*, 47-ft aluminum, side gates, walk-through transom, large swim-step and platform, hot showers, differential GPS and plotter, auto pilot, scanning sonar, video fathometer,VHF radio and radar, 20 passengers
Trips: Day-trips to Coronados
Courses: None

Northern Cortez Region

Charters Mar de Cortez

Mail: Mike Sullivan, El Dorado Ranch,
P.O. Box 9018, Calexico, CA 92232, U.S.
☎ 657-71278 fax: 657-71779
Sales: None Rentals: Full
Air: One portable, can be rented

Credit cards: Visa, MasterCard
Courses: Open Water, Advanced Open Water, Medic/First Aid, Rescue Diver, Divemaster
Comments: No boats, specializes in van trips (requires two days' advance notice) and beach dives

San Franciscuito Resort

Mail: 667 Twining Avenue, San Diego,
CA 92154, U.S.
☎ 619-690-1000
Sales: None **Rentals:** Tanks and weight belts
Air: One compressor on premises

Credit cards: None
Boats: Panga rentals available
Comments: The resort has cabins, RV parking, restaurant, showers, rest rooms, an airstrip, gasoline, mechanic and a sand beach

Southern Cortez Region

Aqua Sports de Loreto

Club de Playa, Eden Loreto Resort, Loreto,
BCS, México
Mail: Apdo. Postal 194, Loreto,
BCS, México
☎ 113-30700 fax: 113-30377
aquasports@hotmail.com
www.loreto.com
Sales: None **Rentals:** Full
Air: Two compressors on premises, one portable

Credit cards: Visa, MasterCard
Boats: Pangas from hotel fleet
Trips: Islas los Coronados, Danzante and Carmen
Courses: Open Water, Advanced Open Water, Divemaster, Night, Search & Recovery, Deep, Boat, Navigator, Naturalist, Rescue
Comments: A day-pass to the resort costs $35, and includes breakfast, lunch, cocktails, and equipment rental

Arturo's Sports Fishing Fleet

Paseo Hidalgo s/n, Loreto, BCS, México
Mail: Apdo. Postal 5, Loreto, BCS, México
☎ 113-50766 fax: 113-50022
Sales: None **Rentals:** Full

Air: One compressor on premises
Credit cards: Visa, MasterCard
Boats: Pangas
Trips: Local islands **Courses:** None

Baja Diving & Service

1665 Obregón, La Paz, BCS, México
Mail: Apdo. Postal 782, La Paz, BCS, México
☎ 112-21826 fax: 112-28644
bajadiving@lapaz.cromwell.com.mx
www.trybaja.com/clubcantamar/
Sales: Full **Rentals:** Full
Air: Five compressors, large one on premises
Credit cards: All major cards
Boats: Eleven, ranging from 22-ft pangas to a

42-ft cruiser
Trips: North to Isla San Francisco, east and south to Isla Cerralvo
Courses: Open Water, Divemaster, Deep, Night
Comments: Recompression chamber on premises. Can do VIP and hydrostat. Operates Club Hotel Cantamar. Marina Pichilingue, adjacent to Cantamar, has slips and a boat ramp, open to the public for a small fee

Baja Expeditions

2625 Garnet Avenue, San Diego, CA 92109, U.S.
☎ 619-581-3311 fax: 619-581-6542
Toll-free ☎ 800-843-6967
travel@bajaex.com
www.bajaex.com
Sales: None **Rentals:** Full
Air: Compressor on premises at La Paz facility
Credit cards: MasterCard and Visa for deposit only

Boats: *Rio Rita*, 50 ft, 14-ft beam, on-board compressor, 18 passengers, May through November
Trips: North to Loreto, east and south to Cerralvo
Courses: Open Water referrals only
Comments: One of the largest and oldest adventure travel companies in Baja. Operates live-aboard *Don José*. The office is located near the intersection of Av. Abasolo and Av. Sonora in La Paz

Baja Outpost

Blvd. Lopéz Mateos s/n, Loreto, BCS, México
Mail: Apdo. Postal 52, Loreto, BCS, México
☎/fax: 113-51134 Toll-free ☎ 888-649-5951
bajaoutpost@bajaoutpost.com
www.bajaoutpost.com
Sales: None **Rentals:** Full
Air: Two compressors on premises

Credit cards: All major cards
Boats: A 26-ft and several 22-ft pangas, inflatables
Trips: All local dive sites
Courses: Open Water, Advanced, Rescue, Divemaster, Assistant Instructor, Photographer, Navigator, Night, Search & Recovery, Naturalist
Comments: Operates a bed-and-breakfast

Beach Club El Tecolote

Mail: Dominguez y 5 de Mayo, La Paz, BCS, Méx.
☎ 112-28885 fax: 112-54971
Sales: None **Rentals:** Basic, in limited supply
Air: None on premises, rents full tanks
Credit cards: All major cards
Boats: One 22-ft panga

Trips: Local sites **Courses:** None
Comments: One of the smaller dive operations in
the area, but close to fine diving north of La Paz.
Drive east through La Paz on Av. Abasolo. The
road will curve north and pass the ferry terminal.
At KM 23, take the right fork to the beach

Centro de Buceo Carey

Marquez de León y Topete 2415-A Loc. 17,
Col. el Manglito, La Paz BCS, México
☎/fax: 112-32333
buceocarey@bajanet.mx
Sales: Full **Rentals:** Full, good condition
Air: One compressor on premises, plus a rental
Credit cards: All major cards
Boats: One 22-ft panga, rents a 26-ft panga.
Both have ladders and radios

Trips: All local sites
Courses: Open Water, Advanced Open
Water, Night/Limited Visibility, Search &
Recovery, Stress & Rescue, Open Water
Instructor, Deep Diving, Multi-Level, Tides
& Currents, Instructor
Comments: $2/tank charge for recompression
chamber. The office is in a business complex at
the northwest end of Av. León

Cortez Club (La Paz)

KM 5, Carretera a Pichilingue, La Paz,
BCS, México
☎ 112-16120 fax: 112-16123
thecortezclub@lapaz.cromwell.com.mx
www.cortezclub.com
Sales: Full
Rentals: Full, including lights, DIN fittings for
Europeans, dive computers with air-integration
Air: Two compressors on premises, two portables

Credit cards: All major cards
Boats: Eight, ranging from 22-ft pangas to a
38-ft cruiser
Trips: All local sites, trips on live-aboard *Mariana*.
Courses: All to Instructor, Boat, Deep, Dry Suit,
Multi-level, Navigator, Search & Rescue, Natural-
ist, Wreck
Comments: Diver bar, fresh-water showers, gear
storage. Can do VIP, tank-cleaning

Cortez Explorers

Moctezuma 75A, Mulegé
BCS, México
☎/fax: 115-30500
www.cortez-explorer.com
Sales: None **Rentals:** Full
Air: One compressor on premises
Credit cards: Visa, MasterCard
Boats: One fast, twin-engine 20-ft,

6 divers maximum
Trips: Santa Inéz, Punta Concepción, east coast
of Península Concepción
Courses: Resort course
Comments: The original Mulegé Divers has bro-
keninto two separate businesses, Cortez Explorers
and The Shop (see listing below). Cortez Explorers
provides the facilities and services shown here

Deportes Blazer

Hidalgo 23, Loreto, BCS, México
☎/fax: 113-50911
Sales: Masks, snorkels, fins, small parts
Rentals: Full

Air: One compressor on premises
Credit cards: All major cards
Boats: Twin-engine 21-ft Zodiac to local islands
Courses: None

La Paz Diving Service

Calle Nayarit 10, La Paz, BCS, México
Mail: Apdo. Postal 133, La Paz, BCS, México
☎ 112-23761 fax: 112-56228
marisla@balandra.uabcs.mx
www.pe.net/~marisla

Sales: None **Rentals:** Full
Air: Aboard *Marisla II* **Credit cards:** None
Trips: Operates live-aboard *Marisla II*
Courses: None
Comments: Open May 1 until November 1

Scu-Baja Diving Center (La Paz)

Bravo e/ Mutualismo s/n, Col. Centro, La Paz,
BCS, México
☎ 112-32770 fax: 112-27423
Sales: Full **Rentals:** Full
Air: One installed compressor, one portable

Credit cards: All major cards
Boats: Two 28-ft boats with diesel engines, fully
equipped, 12 divers per boat
Trips: El Bajo, Los Islotes, *Salvatierra*, Cerralvo
Courses: Open Water, Rescue Diver, Night

Scuba Baja Joe

Av. Alvaro Obregón 460, La Paz, BCS, México
Mail: Apdo. Postal 361, Admon. Correos 1,
La Paz, BCS, México
☎ 112-24006 fax: 112-24000
Sales: None **Rentals:** Full

Air: Not on premises, four hours required
Credit cards: Visa, MasterCard
Boats: Pangas with 135 h.p. to 200 h.p. engines
Trips: Cerralvo and all sites north to Ánimas Sur
Courses: All to Assistant Instructor, Night, Naturalist

The Shop

Gral. Martínez s/n, Mulegé, BCS, México
☎/fax: 115-30059
Sales: Basic scuba and snorkeling equipment
Rentals: Full **Air:** None
Credit cards: Visa, MasterCard

Comments: The original Mulegé Divers has broken into two separate businesses, The Shop and
Cortez Explorers (see listing above). The Shop
provides the sales and rentals shown here, as well
as books, T-shirts, fishing equipment

The Cape Region

Amigos del Mar

Blvd. Marina s/n, Cabo San Lucas, BCS, México
Mail: Apdo. Postal 43, Cabo San Lucas,
BCS, México
☎ 114-30505 fax: 114-30887
Toll-free ☎ 800-344-3349
www.amigosdelmar.com
Sales: None **Rentals:** Full
Air: One compressor on premises
Credit cards: Visa, MasterCard

Boats: *Amigo I*, a 33-ft trimaran; *Gran
Amigo*, a 36-ft trimaran, both with toilets;
a 25-ft, twin-engine panga; and a 22-ft panga
Trips: Pulmo, Gorda, Land's End, Santa María
Courses: Open Water, Advanced Open Water,
Rescue, Divemaster, Boat, Night, Naturalist
Comments: $2/tank charge for recompression
chamber. Manages dive operations on *Solmar V*.
Office located at south end of inner boat harbor

Baja Dive Adventures

Mail: Apdo. Postal 50, Buena Vista, BCS, México
☎/fax: 114-10271 Toll-free ☎ 800-533-8452
mrbill@windriders.com
www.windriders.com/baja
Sales: Used rental gear only
Rentals: Full, including air-integrated computers
Air: One compressor on premises
Credit cards: Visa, MasterCard

Boats: 22- and 24-ft pangas equipped with radios
Trips: Pulmo, Cerralvo, many others
Courses: Open Water
Comments: Turn east on the road across from the
PEMEX off the highway at KM 107+ in Los Barriles
and follow the dive flags. Package trips are offered,
walk-ins are welcome. Operates Casa Miramar,
which caters specifically to divers and snorkelers

Baja Dive Expeditions

Plaza las Glorias, Local 1-4, Cabo San Lucas,
BCS, México
☎/fax: 114-33830
bajadive@cabonet.net.mx
www.caboland.com/bajadive/index.html
Sales: None **Rentals:** Full
Air: One compressor not on premises
Credit cards: All major cards

Boats: Three 26-ft whale boats with diesel
engines; a 26-ft SeaRay inboard/outboard; a
24-ft Bayliner with 225 h.p. outboard; and a 22-ft
panga, all with shade, radios, first aid, oxygen
Trips: Pulmo and all local sites
Courses: Open Water, Advanced, Divemaster
Comments: $2/tank charge for recompression
chamber

Cabo Acuadeportes

Mail: Apdo. Postal 136, Cabo San Lucas, BCS, México
☎/fax: 114-30117
cabo@sierra-computers.com
www.sierra-computers.com/~cabo
Sales: Snorkeling **Rentals:** Full
Air: On-premises compressors
Credit cards: All major cards

Boats: Two 26-ft pangas, one 22-ft panga, with radios and safety equipment
Trips: Boat dives only at Hacienda
Courses: By reservation
Comments: Two locations, one at Hotel Hacienda in Cabo San Lucas, the other at Chileno. $2/tank charge for recompression chamber

Cabo Pulmo Divers

☎ 114-71804
Sales: None
Rentals: Full, including computers
Air: Portable, on premises
Credit cards: MasterCard, American Express
Boats: Three 22-ft pangas, one 24-ft, one 26-ft
Trips: Pulmo and vicinity

Courses: None
Comments: Turn northeast at KM 91+ on the Transpeninsular, 57 miles south of La Paz. At KM 10+, turn southeast and set odometer. The pavement ends at mile 10.4, but the gravel road is well-graded. Follow it to Pulmo at mile 16.3

J & R Baja Divers (Cabo San Lucas)

Plaza Bonita Mall 48, Cabo San Lucas, BCS, México
☎/fax: 114-31545
j&rbajadivers@cabotel.com.mx
www.cabotel.com.mx/j&rbajadivers/home.html
Sales: Snorkels, small parts **Rentals:** Full
Air: One on-premises compressor

Credit cards: Cash or traveler's check suggested
Boats: A 23-ft and a 32-ft cruiser
Trips: Divers decide, will go anywhere
Courses: All except Instructor; Deep, Dry-Suit, Night, Boat, Search & Recovery, Naturalist
Comments: Hotel and dive packages available. Ask about the new "Eighteen-Hole" site

Land's End Divers

Plaza las Glorias, Local A-5, Cabo San Lucas, BCS, México
☎/fax: 114-32200 Toll-free ☎ 800-675-3483
bajatec1@cabonet.net.mx
www.mexonline.com/landsend.htm
Sales: None **Rentals:** Full
Air: One compressor, not on premises

Credit cards: American Express
Boats: One 22-ft dive boat, with 130 h.p. engine
Trips: All local sites, Pulmo, Gorda
Courses: Open Water, Advanced Open Water, Divemaster, Medic/First Aid, Rescue Diver
Comments: Disabled divers welcome. $2/tank charge for recompression chamber

Neptune Divers

Plaza las Glorias Local A-14, Cabo San Lucas, BCS, México
☎/fax: 114-31110
Sales: Masks, snorkels, fins
Rentals: Full
Air: One compressor not on premises
Credit cards: American Express, Visa

Boats: 27-ft panga with radio
Trips: Sandfalls, Pelican Rock, Neptune's Finger, Santa María, Chileno, Gorda, Pulmo, others
Courses: Open Water, Advanced Open Water, Rescue, Divemaster
Comments: $2/tank charge for recompression chamber

Pacific Coast Adventures

Plaza las Glorias, Local H-6, Cabo San Lucas, BCS, México
☎ 114-31070 fax: 114-31560
pcatemo@cabonet.net.mx
www.pacificcoastadv.com
Sales: Regulators
Rentals: Full
Air: Compressor at warehouse near office
Credit cards: All major cards
Boats: One custom 29-ft, three custom 23-ft boats

Trips: All local sites
Courses: All basic certifications, Deep, Enriched Air, Equipment Specialist, Multi-Level, Navigator, Night, Peak Performance, Buoyancy, Research, Search & Recovery, Naturalist, Photographer, Wreck
Comments: $2/tank charge for recompression chamber. Will arrange dive tours, most dive guides are Assistant Instructors. Underwater housings available for disposable cameras

Pepe's Dive Center

Mail: Apdo. Postal 532, Cabo San Lucas,
BCS, México
☎/fax: 114-10001 Toll-free ☎ 800-246-6226
pepe@crossadventure.com
www.crossadventure.com/pepe
Sales: BCs, regulators, masks, snorkels, fins,
wet suits, small parts, etc. Rentals: Full
Air: One compressor on premises
Credit cards: Visa, MasterCard
Boats: Two 22-ft pangas

Trips: Pulmo, El Cantil, sea lion colony between
Cabo Pulmo and Los Frailes
Courses: All to Divemaster; Deep, Naturalist,
Night, Wreck
Comments: Rents two cabins with kitchens, hot
water. Turn northeast on the paved road at KM
91+ on the Transpeninsular, 57 miles south of La
Paz. At KM 10+, turn southeast and set odometer.
The pavement ends at mile 10.4, but the gravel
road is well graded. Arrive at Pulmo at mile 16.3

Tío Sports

Mail: Apdo. Postal 37, Cabo San Lucas,
BCS, México
☎ 114-32986 fax 114-31521
Toll-free ☎ 800-246-6226
tiosport@cabonet.net.mx
www.tiosports.com/menu.html
Sales: None Rentals: Full
Air: One compressor on premises
Credit cards: All major cards

Boats: One 24-ft panga, one 26-ft custom panga,
a 26-ft cruiser, a 32-ft platform boat
Trips: All local sites, Pulmo, Gorda
Courses: All to Divemaster; Deep, Multi-Level,
Naturalist, Night
Comments: $2/tank charge for recompression
chamber. Has reservation desks at the Hotels Marina
Fiesta, Meliá Cabo Real, Meliá San Lucas, Palmilla,
and Westin Regina, and a facility at Playa Médano.

Underwater Diversions

Plaza las Glorias Local F-5, Marina Blvd. s/n,
Cabo San Lucas, BCS, México
☎/fax: 114-34004 Toll-free ☎ 800-342-3143
divecabo@sure.net
www.divecabo.com
Sales: Wetsuits, masks, snorkels, regulators
Rentals: Full, including lights
Air: One compressor on premises

Credit cards: Visa, MasterCard
Boats: *Marisela*, a twin-engine custom dive boat
with freshwater showers, head, ladders, tank
racks, shade and sun deck, up to 20 divers and
50 tanks
Courses: Open Water to Divemaster; Boat, Navigator, Night, Search & Recovery, Video, Wreck
Comments: Repairs regulators. $2/tank charge for
recompression chamber.

Vista Sea Sports

Mail: Apdo. Postal 42, Buena Vista BCS, México
☎/fax: 114-10031 Toll-free ☎ 800-368-4334
Sales: Masks, snorkels, fins. Occasional rental
equipment Rentals: Full
Air: Two compressors on premises.
Credit cards: Visa, MasterCard
Boats: *Shamrock* 22-ft diesel cruiser, two 23-ft
super-pangas with 115 h.p. Evinrudes, one 22-ft
commercial panga with a 55 h.p. outboard, radio

full USCG equipment, depth finders on all boats
Trips: Pulmo, all local dive sites
Courses: All through Divemaster; Deep, Naturalist,
Photographer
Comments: Turn east at from the highway at
KM 103+ in the town of Los Barriles, pass the
hotel, turn right (south) at the two white build-
ings, and look for a white house with green trim
sporting the diver's flag

Live-Aboards

Don José

Home port: La Paz
Description: 80-ft, 18-ft beam, single diesel, wood hull
Equipment: Radar, SSB, VHF, depth finder, twin compressors, electrical power
Accommodations: Seven air conditioned staterooms, three freshwater showers
Destinations: Throughout southern Cortez
Duration: 8 days, at sea 6 nights
Season: May through November
Passengers: 16
Contact: Baja Expeditions

Horizon

Home port: San Diego
Description: 80-ft, 25-ft beam, twin V-12 diesels, twin generators*
Equipment: Water-makers, complete electronics and safety equipment, on-board compressors, swim platforms, underwater recall system
Accommodations: Two air-conditioned bunkrooms, restrooms, hot showers, galley, salon, clothes dryer, wetsuit/drying room, sun deck, and areas for maintenance and camera storage
Destinations: Baja's Pacific Coast
Duration: 5 to 12 days
Season: June through October
Passengers: 31
Contact: Horizon Charters
Comments: SOLAS-equipped and licensed for diving ventures up to 160 miles south of Cabo San Lucas

Maríana

Home port: La Paz
Description: 56-ft motor yacht
Equipment: Radar, depth sounder, GPS, radio, on-board compressor
Accommodations: Large stern cabin, two smaller cabins, hot showers, large living area, lots of deck space on three levels
Destinations: North to Loreto, south to Pulmo and Gorda
Duration: 3 to 10 days
Season: All year
Passengers: 6
Contact: Cortez Club

Marisla II

Home port: La Paz
Description: 121' x 25' x 7' draft, 325 tons
Equipment: GPS, fathometer, weather fax, side-band radio capable of world-wide communications
Accommodations: Eight staterooms, rooms outside
Destinations: Throughout southern Cortez
Duration: 7 to 11 days
Season: May through November
Passengers: 16
Contact: La Paz Diving Service
Comments: Ex-U.S. Coast Guard Cutter *Columbine*

Solmar V

Home port: Cabo San Lucas
Description: 112-ft luxury yacht, 2 diesel main engines, 11 knots, 3 diesel generators, 2 water-makers
Equipment: Side-scanning sonar, radar systems, two air compressors with cascade storage
Accommodations: Mahogany interior, televisions, galley, air conditioned, 12 staterooms with private bathrooms, sink, shower, color TV and VCR
Destinations: *Socorro* 9 days, November through June; *Clarion* twice a year, November and March, 11 days; Sea of Cortez July through October, 8 days; Pulmo once a year, August, 5 days
Passengers: 22
Contact: Cabo Resort Reservations
Comments: Serves three meals, soft drinks, beer and wine with meals, tanks and weights; can rent additional equipment from Amigos del Mar. Manta Ray Awareness course available.

---

* See also *Ocean Odyssey*, operated by Horizon Charters, page 146.

Publications

Behrens, David W., *Pacific Coast Nudibranchs, A Guide to the Opisthobranchs, Alaska to Baja California.* Monterey (CA): Sea Challengers, 1991. Some of the most colorful and spectacular living organisms on earth come in the unlikely forms of the gelatinous, slug-like nudibranchs. Don't miss this book if you are a diver with a taste for the small, the flamboyant, and the beautiful.

Bernhardson, Wayne. *Baja California.* Hawthorn (Victoria): Lonely Planet, 1998. An excellent general guide to the peninsula.

Brusca, Richard C., *Common Intertidal Invertebrates of the Gulf of California.* Tucson: University of Arizona Press, 1980. A scholarly handbook, with numerous photos and sketches and an extensive bibliography.

Gotshall, Daniel W., *Marine Animals of Baja California.* Monterey (CA): Sea Challengers, 1982. An excellent guide to the fish and marine invertebrates, illustrated by many color photographs.

Gotshall, Daniel W., *Sea of Cortez Marine Animals.* Monterey (CA): Sea Challengers, 1998. In 112 pages, this fine new book describes 190 species of fish and 112 invertebrates, all of them illustrated by color photos.

Kerstitch, Alex, *Sea of Cortez Marine Invertebrates.* Monterey (CA): Sea Challengers, 1989. A beautiful, full-color review of the sponges, hydroids, anemones, gorgonians, worms, clams, oysters, nudibranchs, slugs, octopus, shrimp, crabs, sea stars, and other critters often seen but rarely known by divers and snorkelers.

Peterson, Walt and Michael Peterson, *Exploring Baja by RV.* Berkeley: Wilderness Press, 1996. The only guide written specifically for those traveling by recreational vehicle, this excellent guide provides everything you need to know to have an enjoyable, safe, and inexpensive vacation in Baja.

Peterson, Walt, *The Baja Adventure Book.* Berkeley: Wilderness Press, 1998. For a variety of outdoor activities, this book is easily the best choice.

Thomson, Donald A., Lloyd T. Findley and Alex N. Kerstitch, *Reef Fishes of the Sea of Cortez.* New York: John Wiley & Sons, 1979. One of the best guides available to the many reef fishes seen by scuba divers and snorkelers in the Cortez.

Wrobel, David, and Claudia Mills, *Pacific Coast Pelagic Invertebrates—A Guide to the Common Gelatinous Animals.* Monterey (CA): Sea Challengers, 1998. This pioneering field guide describes 95 species of jellies, 27 species of comb jellies, 24 species of pelagic mollusks, and 20 species of pelagic tunicates, each species illustrated by a color photo.

Index

dive sites covered in this book appear in **bold** type

Lonely Planet Series Descriptions

Lonely Planet **travel guides** explore a destination in depth with options to suit a range of budgets. With reliable, practical advice on getting around, restaurants and accommodations, these easy-to-use guides also include detailed maps, color photographs, extensive background material and coverage of sites both on and off the beaten track.

For budget travelers **shoestring guides** are the best single source of travel information covering an entire continent or large region. Written by experienced travelers these 'tried and true' classics offer reliable, first-hand advice on transportation, restaurants and accommodations, and insider tips for avoiding bureaucratic confusion and stretching money as far as possible.

City guides cover many of the world's great cities with full-color photographs throughout, front and back cover gatefold maps, and information for every traveler's budget and style. With information for business travelers, all the best places to eat and shop and itinerary suggestions for long and short-term visitors, city guides are a complete package.

Lonely Planet **phrasebooks** have essential words and phrases to help travelers communicate with the locals. With color tabs for quick reference, an extensive vocabulary, use of local scripts and easy-to-follow pronunciation instructions, these handy, pocket-sized language guides cover most situations a traveler is likely to encounter.

Lonely Planet **walking guides** cover some of the world's most exciting trails. With detailed route descriptions including degrees of difficulty and best times to go, reliable maps and extensive background information, these guides are an invaluable resource for both independent hikers and those in organized groups.

Lonely Planet **travel atlases** are thoroughly researched and fact-checked by the guidebook authors to ensure they complement the books. And the handy format means none of the holes, wrinkles, tears, or constant folding and refolding of flat maps. They include background information in five languages.

Journeys is a new series of travel literature that captures the spirit of a place, illuminates a culture, recounts an adventure and introduces a fascinating way of life. Written by a diverse group of writers, they are tales to read while on the road or at home in your favorite armchair.

Entertaining, independent and adventurous, Lonely Planet **videos** encourage the same approach to travel as the guidebooks. Currently broadcast throughout the world, this award-winning series features all original footage and music.

Lonely Planet Pisces Books

The **Diving & Snorkeling** books are dive guides to top destinations worldwide. Beautifully illustrated with full-color photos throughout, the series explores the best diving and snorkeling areas and prepares divers for what to expect when they get there. Each site is described in detail, with information on suggested ability levels, depth, visibility, and, of course, marine life. There's basic topside information as well for each destination. Don't miss the guides to:

Australia: Coral Sea &
  Great Barrier Reef

Australia: Southeast Coast

Bahamas: Family Islands & Grand

Bahamas: Nassau &
  New Providence

Baja

Bali & the Komodo Region

Belize

Bermuda

Best Caribbean Diving

Bonaire

British Virgin Islands

Cayman Islands

Cocos Island

Cozumel

Cuba

Curaçao

Fiji

Florida Keys

Florida's East Coast

Guam & Yap

Hawaiian Islands

Jamaica

Northern California
  & Monterey Peninsula

Pacific Northwest

Palau

Puerto Rico

Red Sea

Roatan & Honduras'
  Bay Islands

Scotland

Seychelles

Southern California

St. Maarten, Saba,
  & St. Eustatius

Texas

Truk Lagoon

Turks & Caicos

U.S. Virgin Islands

Vanuatu

Plus illustrated natural history guides:

Pisces Guide to Caribbean
  Reef Ecology

Great Reefs of the World

Sharks of Tropical &
  Temperate Seas

Venomous & Toxic
  Marine Life of
  the World

Watching Fishes

Where to Find Us . . .

Lonely Planet is known worldwide for publishing practical, reliable and no-nonsense travel information in our guides and on our web site. The Lonely Planet list covers just about every accessible part of the world. Currently there are nine series: *Pisces books, travel guides, shoestring guides, walking guides, city guides, phrasebooks, audio packs, travel atlases* and *Journeys*–a unique collection of travel writing.

Lonely Planet Publications

Australia
PO Box 617, Hawthorn 3122, Victoria
☎ (03) 9819 1877 fax (03) 9819 6459
e-mail talk2us@lonelyplanet.com.au

USA
150 Linden Street
Oakland, California 94607
☎ (510) 893 8555, (800) 275 8555
fax (510) 893 8563
e-mail info@lonelyplanet.com

UK
10A Spring Place,
London NW5 3BH
☎ (0171) 428 4800 fax (0171) 428 4828
e-mail go@lonelyplanet.co.uk

France
1 rue du Dahomey
75011 Paris
☎ 01 55 25 33 00 fax 01 55 25 33 01
e-mail bip@lonelyplanet.fr

World Wide Web: www.lonelyplanet.com or **AOL keyword: lp**